essential ECONOMICS

essential

ECONOMICS

ADRIAN LYONS

Hodder & Stoughton

A MEMBER OF THE HODDER HEADLINE GROUP

British Library Cataloguing in Publication Data

Lyons, Adrian
Essential economics
1. Economics
I. Title
330

ISBN 0 340 68344 9

First published 1996

Impression number	10 9 8 7 6 5 4 3 2 1
Year	1999 1998 1997 1996

Typeset by Wearset, Boldon, Tyne and Wear.
Printed in Great Britain for Hodder & Stoughton Educational, a division of Hodder Headline Plc, 338 Euston Road, London NW1 3BH by Bath Press

To Jacqui

Contents

Advanced Level GNVQ Business Unit 1 (Business in the Economy)

The following units will be of particular interest to students following Advanced Level GNVQ Business Unit 1 (Business in the Economy):

Element		*Chapter number*	*Chapter title*
1.1	**Analyse the forces of supply and demand on business**	**4**	**Demand**
		5	**Supply**
		6	**Price**
		7	**Elasticity**
1.2	**Analyse the operation of markets and their effects on businesses and communities**	**11**	**Business ownership**
		12	**The aims of business**
		13	**The benefits of competition**
		17	**Monopolies: good or bad?**
		18	**The environment: are externalities a necessary evil?**
1.3	**Examine the effects of government policies on markets**	**15**	**Public and merit goods**
		16	**Privatisation**
		19	**When should governments intervene in markets?**

Acknowledgements

Many thanks must go to my wife Jacqui for her patient support while this book was being written, and for her useful comments on the manuscript. Thanks also to Richard Young (formerly Education and Marketing Director of the Economics and Business Education Association) for his helpful comments and support.

The author and publishers would also like to thank the following for permission to use material in this text:

The Guardian; Times Newspapers Ltd; Eurostat; Renault UK Limited; The Telegraph plc; The Salvation Army, and the Office for National Statistics.

Doing economics

What is economics about?

Here's a puzzle. In the American state of Washington, along its northern border with Canada, small piles of clothes are found in local car parks. Why is this?

What has this puzzle got to do with economics? This may well be a more obvious question. Well, the solution to the puzzle can be found at the end of this chapter, but at this stage I will give you a clue: the solution has *everything* to do with economics. Actually, more things than you might think are connected with economics. Let's pick up one newspaper on one day and look at the front page. You can do it today. I did it on Wednesday 19 April 1995. The paper I chose was *The Guardian*, and these were the headlines on the front page:

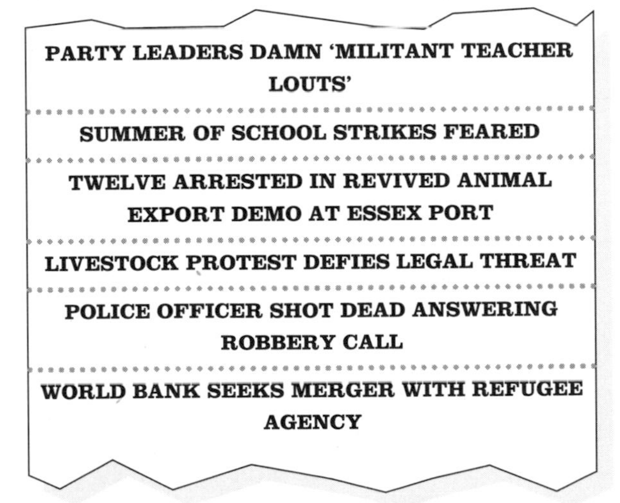
PARTY LEADERS DAMN 'MILITANT TEACHER LOUTS'

SUMMER OF SCHOOL STRIKES FEARED

TWELVE ARRESTED IN REVIVED ANIMAL EXPORT DEMO AT ESSEX PORT

LIVESTOCK PROTEST DEFIES LEGAL THREAT

POLICE OFFICER SHOT DEAD ANSWERING ROBBERY CALL

WORLD BANK SEEKS MERGER WITH REFUGEE AGENCY

Perhaps the last of these headlines is the only one that you would think of as dealing with economics because it mentions a bank, but in fact all of these stories are centred on economics. Teachers were threatening strike action because of the limited amount of money being spent on education – an economics issue. The spring of 1995 saw protests around the UK, notably at Shoreham in Sussex and Brightlingsea in Essex, aimed at preventing the export of young calves to be reared in France, Belgium and the Netherlands. Again, several economics issues were raised: farmers would receive less income if the calves were not exported; transport businesses needed the customers; and because money was being spent by Sussex and Essex police forces to keep many officers at the ports so as to ensure the movement of the calves, that same money was unavailable for spending on other police work such as crime detection or prevention. Even the story concerning the murdered police officer concerns an economics issue, because he was attending a robbery where a criminal thought that the extra money he could get from the robbery was worth killing for. (Generally, while many people dislike aspects of the way our economic system provides different amounts of money to different people, most people do not, however, commit violent crime to change their situation!)

Using this book

This book is different from other economics textbooks in several ways. First, it is smaller than most textbooks. That is because it tries to explain only the central concepts of the subject, and to show how they help us to explain the world in which we live. After reading parts of this book, you may wish to use the library to explore issues in more detail. That's fine, and I would encourage you to do that, but always remember that you can return to this book for a clear explanation of the issue. While other books go into greater depth, that depth can be confusing. This book aims to give clear explanations that will help you to understand the real issues and the theories that explain economic problems, together with proposed solutions.

A common feature of economics textbooks is the use of diagrams. Economists like diagrams, especially ones that appear difficult to understand. This makes economics appear difficult, and if economics is difficult, then anyone who can do it must be very clever. That is what economists would like you to believe. I strongly disagree with this. Whilst economics exams may be difficult, understanding economics is quite straightforward. A second point, therefore, is that this book uses few diagrams. There are some, but only where it is 'essential', and I have tried to make them clear and simple to understand.

Economists also try to make themselves appear exclusive by using a language that does not make sense to the general public. Terms are used which can be very off-putting, but really they are special 'economics speak' for what is common sense. I have tried to use ordinary English as much as possible, but sometimes you do need to know the 'economics speak'. However, where this has been used, it is always either explained or given an English translation.

Chapter style

Each chapter is introduced with some historical background. This sets out a real-life economic problem, and the chapter will go on to explain how economists have dealt with it. Do not skip these sections: they show you what economics is all about. It is not about theories and diagrams: it is about real-world issues such as poverty, unemployment, the funding for the health service or education etc.

Economics as a social science

Economics is a member of a group of subjects that try to understand the way society operates. It is like science subjects such as physics or chemistry in that people try to come up with the best explanation for what can be observed happening. In chemistry, two chemicals can be mixed together and a reaction takes place. Chemists use what they know about the way molecules interact to explain the change of colour that takes place (if that, for example, is the chemical reaction).

If you remember chemistry experiments at school, you will recall that you could never be sure that if you were watching two chemicals react, it wasn't something other than the two chemicals that affected the reaction – perhaps there was something in the atmosphere. Chemists can try to cut out such possibilities by conducting experiments in a vacuum. This is clearly something that social scientists *cannot* do. Social scientists such as economists can only observe the world as it is, and make statements about what they think causes things. They can never *isolate* the things they are studying, and this means there could always be something else affecting the results. That is why economics uses the Latin phrase *ceteris paribus*, meaning 'if everything else stays the same', when describing what they expect to happen.

Why economists disagree

Even in physics, you can find disagreement amongst scientists. We are often led to believe at school that science is a set of agreed facts and an agreed understanding about the way the world works. If this were the case, however, scientists wouldn't need to spend so much time on research trying to find better explanations for the workings of the universe. Economists too try to find better explanations in the face of new facts. For example, until the 1930s, the agreed wisdom of economists was that unemployment was caused by wages being too high. Then, in the 1930s, what were already very high levels of unemployment in the UK continued to increase, while wages fell. According to accepted economics theory, this shouldn't happen. A new group of economists (**Keynesian**) therefore argued that cutting wages made unemployment worse. The way to reduce unemployment was now to increase spending. This was a better theory to fit the facts. An increase in spending in the lead up to World War II (1939–1945) did eradicate the unemployment problem, and so Keynesianism was seen as the solution to unemployment, until the 1970s and 1980s when high levels of unemployment were again a major problem. Once again, a better theory was sought, and this led to **supply side analysis**: the view that unemployment was due not to a lack of demand but rather to the fact that workers were too expensive and poorly trained, and that rules and regulations discouraged employers from taking on more workers.

Whenever there is new thinking about an issue, many economists will disagree about it. This is because economic theories are based on assumptions about how people behave. If we could be sure about answers to questions like the following, then we could predict what will happen.

- How will people respond to a price rise?
- How will people respond to a cut in pay?
- How will people respond to a cut in welfare benefits?
- How will people respond to a cut in their taxes?
- How will people respond to an increase in interest rates?

What would your answers be to those questions? You can probably make rough guesses, but really you need more information (the price of *what*? What *sort* of taxes?). Even when given more information, economists can only say that people have behaved like this in the past, but their behaviour might *change* in the future – because we are dealing, after all, with people. In the mid-1990s, interest rates were relatively low and unemployment was falling. Based on previous experience, people should have increased their spending on goods in the shops. However, increases in spending were very small, and much less than would be expected. The Conservative government of John Major anxiously waited for the so called 'feel-good factor', for the time when people would feel optimistic about their financial future, but this didn't come, although the 'economic indicators' said it should have been there. Economists cannot therefore predict people's feelings.

Economics and the real world

The next statement may seem ridiculously obvious, but 'Economics is about the economy'. The economy is reported every day on the news, in the papers and on current-affairs programmes. If you are following an exam course, it is vital that you use the media to keep up to date with economic issues: all textbooks are *out of date* by the time they are published, because events in economics are constantly changing.

Summary

Economics attempts to explain the way the world works. In economics, there are competing views, and you need to choose the best explanation to fit the facts. There are many sources of further study that are interesting and easily available. Always remember that economics is about *people* and their *well-being*.

Solution to puzzle

Clothes were much cheaper in the USA than in Canada. When people in Canada needed new clothes, they would therefore drive over the border to buy their clothes from a store in the USA, provided they lived close enough to the border to make this worthwhile. However, Canada charged high taxes on people bringing home goods that they had bought in the USA. To get around this, people from Canada would wear old clothes on their cross-border journey to the shops, buy their new clothes in the USA, change into these and throw away their old clothes. They would then cross the border back into Canada, and the customs officials would assume that these Canadians were wearing clothes that they had set off in. That way, no tax could be charged. As approximately three-quarters of the people of Canada inhabit a relatively narrow belt along the US frontier, this has proved a popular way for many Canadians to save money.

Part I

The market economy

Chapter 2

Scarcity and choice

EU jobless rate steady at 10.7%

Unemployment in the European Union remained at 10.7 per cent in September, unchanged from the previous month, Eurostat, the EU's statistics agency, has reported. The rate was unchanged from September 1993. Eurostat estimated that 17.1 million people were unemployed in September, from an EU population of 340 million. The rates have fallen most in Britain, the Republic of Ireland and Denmark during the past year.

(The Times, 22 November 1994)

In 1944, as the UK sensed the coming victory in World War II, the then government published a White Paper on Employment (a **white paper** is the first draft of a law) whose opening sentence states a commitment: 'The government accepts as one of their primary aims and responsibilities the maintenance of a high and stable level of employment after the war.' That commitment was a central policy of governments in industrialised countries for the following 30 years. The last 20 years have seen unemployment levels that were undreamed of during the 1950s and 1960s (see Table 2.1). So is unemployment now the fundamental economic problem?

Table 2.1 Registered unemployed as a percentage of the civilian workforce, 1960–92

	Europe 12	France	Italy	UK	USA	Japan
1960	–	1.4	5.1	1.4	–	–
1961	–	1.2	4.6	1.2	–	–
1962	–	1.4	4.1	1.6	–	–
1963	–	1.5	3.5	1.9	–	–
1964	–	1.2	3.9	1.4	–	–
1965	–	1.5	4.9	1.2	–	–
1966	–	1.6	5.3	1.1	–	–
1967	–	2.1	4.9	1.9	–	–
1968	–	2.6	5.2	2.1	–	–
1969	–	2.3	5.1	2.0	–	–
1970	6.3	2.4	4.9	2.1	–	–
1971	2.5	2.7	4.9	2.7	–	–
1972	3.0	2.8	5.8	3.0	–	–
1973	2.9	2.7	5.8	2.1	–	–
1974	3.0	2.8	4.9	2.0	–	–
1975	4.3	4.0	5.3	3.2	–	–
1976	5.0	4.4	6.1	4.8	–	–
1977	5.4	4.9	6.2	5.1	–	–
1978	5.9	5.1	6.3	5.0	–	–
1979	5.8	5.8	6.6	4.5	–	–
1980	6.0	6.2	6.5	5.5	–	2.0
1981	7.6	7.3	7.3	8.8	7.6	2.2
1982	8.9	8.0	7.9	10.1	9.7	2.4
1983	9.9	8.2	8.7	11.0	9.6	2.6
1984	10.6	9.7	9.3	11.0	7.5	2.7
1985	10.8	10.1	9.6	11.4	7.2	2.6
1986	10.7	10.3	10.5	11.4	7.0	2.8
1987	10.3	10.4	10.3	10.4	6.2	2.8
1988	9.7	9.9	10.8	8.5	5.5	2.3
1989	8.9	9.4	10.6	7.1	5.3	2.3
1990	8.4	9.0	9.8	6.4	5.5	2.1
1991	8.6	9.5	9.4	8.4	6.7	2.2
1992	9.1	10.1	9.5	9.8	6.9	2.2

(EuroStat)

The fundamental economic problem

Here are some examples of economic problems that face many Western countries in the 1990s:

- homelessness
- poverty
- unemployment
- limited money for schools
- limited money for health care

Which of these do you consider the most important? Difficult to choose, isn't it! Are any of the above so important that it causes all of the other problems? If the answer is no, then we must find something else to be our fundamental economic problem that causes all the others.

Economists in fact define the fundamental economic problem as that of 'infinite wants and finite resources'. In other words, while there is no limit to people's wants, the resources available to meet those wants are limited. Obviously, some resources are more limited than others, but there are very few resources in the world that people can have as much of as they want without reducing the amount available for somebody else. Fresh air used to be considered something that was available to everyone without limit, but with increasing levels of pollution this is becoming questionable. Sea water, however, does perhaps fit the bill, and so can be referred to as a **free good**. On the other hand, everything upon which there is a limit is known as an **economic good**. Note that services that we receive for free, such as health care or education, are not free goods: they still have to be paid for in some way.

Economists say that anything that is not a free good is **scarce**. In economics, 'scarce' does not mean 'rare': for something to be scarce, there must be a *limit* to its availability. In economics, **scarcity** means 'limited in supply'. Therefore, as homes are scarce, society has to decide whether everyone should have a home. Similarly, jobs are scarce, so society has to decide whether everyone should have a job.

Economists say that as a result of the fundamental economic problem, there are three further problems that society must address:

1. Decisions need to be made as to *what* to produce, because if workers and machines are being used to make weapons, the same workers and machines cannot be making consumer goods at the same time. This is called the **allocation problem**.
2. Then, decisions need to be made about *how* to produce these goods: should robots be used when there are many people without jobs? This is the **production problem**.
3. Finally, *who* should receive goods and services? Who should have access to high-quality health care? The rich, as in the USA? The most acutely ill? The youngest? This is the **distribution problem**.

Economics cannot answer questions that involve the word 'should'. In a democracy, those questions are for voters to decide. What economics does do is alert people to the questions, and to point out the consequences of the answers. For example, in the mid-1990s, President Clinton in the USA wanted everyone to have access to health care. The consequence would have been that people who already had health-care insurance would have had to pay higher taxes for others to benefit from health care. However, a Republican Congress was elected, committed to preventing health-care reform. In many European countries, on the other hand, people are generally happy to pay taxes to fund a National Health Service.

Economic systems

To some extent, all real economies are mixtures of *theoretical* economies. There are two main types of theoretical economic system, and although no country exactly matches either theory, most countries do tend towards one of the two types of theoretical system: a **command economy** or a **market economy**.

The command economy

A command (or planned) economy is one where the decisions of allocation, production and distribution are decided by the state. The UK was a command economy during World War II as the government directed the output of the economy to meeting the needs of the war. This type of economy is most closely associated, however, with **communism** because it has mainly (although by no means entirely) been used in countries with communist governments. For 40 years up to 1989, therefore, the countries of Central and Eastern Europe, together with the Soviet Union, provided classic examples of command economies. During the 1990s, these countries are all trying to change to market economies, and although communist governments still exist in countries like China, they are becoming less attached to a command system.

In the former Soviet Union in the 1930s, Stalin decided that the main priority for the economy was heavy industry. Resources were targeted at the coal, gas and electricity industries, leaving few resources available for consumer goods. In a command economy, the state owns all the means of production and allocates all the country's output. There are times when this can be very useful: during the 1930s, the former Soviet Union succeeded in achieving Stalin's goal of rapid increases in industrial output; and command economies are also useful in ensuring that available resources are distributed widely around the country, with the result that unemployment, for example, is usually illegal.

The big disadvantage of command economies is as follows. If the state owns all businesses and decides what will be produced, then there is no incentive to develop new ideas or new production methods. There is also, indeed, little incentive for anyone to work hard. The lack of financial incentives leads to low levels of production, and where only the government decides what is produced, consumers have no choice over what they can buy, so that there are actually very *few* resources to be distributed.

The market economy

The market economy, **free enterprise** system or **free market** system (they all mean the same thing) is based on everyone trying to play roles as if they were actors. Each person takes the role of being a **consumer**, while many are also workers. Some people are also **producers** in the sense that they own the businesses that produce the things that consumers want to buy. Each of these roles involves improvisation, but the role-play cards all say the following:

- Consumers will try to buy goods and services as cheaply as they can
- Workers will try to obtain high wages
- Producers will try to charge high prices and pay low wages

Remember that, often, more than one role will be played by the same person. For example, a worker may be pleased with a pay rise but may complain about a price rise introduced to pay for somebody else's pay rise.

There is no economy-wide planning by anybody in this system. Firms need workers to produce goods and services because they are able to make money by selling these goods and services. A person can buy anything that somebody has thought of producing. The only limit is how much money they have. This in turn is determined by what that person can sell. For most people, what they have to sell is their **labour**; and the more skilled their labour is, the more producers will be prepared to pay for it.

Consumers in a market economy have lots of choice as to what to buy, and there is a great incentive for producers to come up with new ideas and better ways of producing so that consumers will buy from *them* rather than from a competitor. In a free market economy, 'signals' are sent between buyers and sellers through the **price mechanism**. (The workings of the price mechanism are explained in Chapters 4–6.)

The big disadvantage with the market-economy system is that some people may not have anything to sell: they might be unable to work through a lack of skills or through there simply being too few jobs available for the number of people available to work. Furthermore, even those people who *are* in work may be unable to afford some of the highly valued services that they need such as health care or education.

There are no examples of pure market economies, but places like Hong Kong and Singapore come quite close.

Mixed economies

As has been said, all economies are mixtures of command and market. In Western Europe, for example, the tradition has been to have a system where the *government* provides for basic needs (often accounting for over 40% of total spending) while all other production and distribution centres use a free market system. In the UK, the Conservative government of the 1980s–1990s had as a main idea **privatisation**. This is a move towards a more market-based system. In 1979, the following major industries were owned and run by the government: telecommunications, gas, electricity, water, steel production, coal and rail. In 1995, a law was introduced to Parliament to sell the last of these (rail) to the private sector, all others already having been privatised.

Within mixed economies, there is often a debate concerning just how far the government should be involved in providing goods and services. It has already been mentioned that in the USA, there has never been an agreement that the government should provide a health service. Here, the government's funding role is very limited – education, law and order (although there are as many private security guards as police), and defence only – and as a result, US taxes are very low compared with Europe; and yet it's a

Table 2.2 Government revenue and spending as a percentage of GDP in the UK and Denmark, 1970–92

	Revenue		Spending	
	UK	Denmark	UK	Denmark
1970	39.7	46.2	36.8	42.1
1971	37.7	46.9	36.4	43.0
1972	36.1	46.5	37.4	42.6
1973	35.3	47.3	38.0	42.1
1974	38.9	49.1	42.7	45.9
1975	39.5	46.8	44.0	48.2
1976	38.6	47.6	43.5	47.8
1977	38.3	48.3	41.5	48.8
1978	36.9	50.3	41.2	50.6
1979	37.7	51.5	41.0	53.2
1980	39.5	52.9	42.9	56.2
1981	41.5	52.9	44.1	59.8
1982	42.1	52.0	44.6	61.2
1983	41.4	54.4	44.7	61.6
1984	41.5	56.2	45.4	60.3
1985	41.4	57.3	44.1	59.3
1986	40.4	59.1	42.8	55.7
1987	39.7	59.7	41.1	57.3
1988	39.3	59.5	38.2	59.0
1989	39.1	58.2	37.9	58.7
1990	38.4	56.1	39.1	57.6
1991	38.1	55.9	40.0	57.5
1992	37.3	55.3	40.9	56.8

(EuroStat)

popular cry by American politicians that the government should do even less and cut taxes still more. Table 2.2 shows how government spending and taxes vary between two countries: the UK and Denmark.

Remember that we said that economics cannot tell us the answer to 'should' questions, so the answers to 'How much should the government spend?' or 'How high should taxes be?' are instead *political* ones. Politicians – but of course, more importantly, *voters* (for example, in the UK and Denmark) – have come to quite different answers. Generally speaking, left-wing political parties (e.g. the British Labour party, the German SDP and the French Socialists) prefer more government spending, while right-wing parties (e.g. the British Conservatives, the German CDU and the French Gaullists) prefer less government spending.

Opportunity cost

As resources are scarce (i.e. limited), choices have to be made about how these resources will be used. If you have 40 pence to spend, you can buy a Mars bar or a Picnic bar, but not both: you would have to choose. Similarly, the government may need to choose between spending £1 billion on a submarine or spending it on a hospital.

Depending on your view of your needs at the time, one of these choices will appear to be the *best choice*, and so if you act rationally that will be your choice. The **opportunity cost** is here defined as the *next best alternative foregone (or gone without)*.

Production possibility frontiers

Resources are limited, and choices have to be made about *what* those resources will be used to produce. Countries that devote a relatively large part of their resources to military production have relatively fewer resources available for consumer goods. These **trade-offs** are illustrated by a **production possibility frontier (or curve)**. Figure 2.1 shows the different combinations of goods that can be produced if all available resources are being used. If all resources are being used for military production, there would be none at all available for consumer goods, and vice versa. Anywhere inside the curve is a point where there are unused resources, and here production of either military or consumer goods could be increased without affecting the other. The opportunity cost of moving from point A to point B (i.e. of increasing military production) would therefore be the loss of the opportunity to make some consumer goods. From point C, on the other hand, military production could be increased without reducing the production of consumer goods: production could just move out towards the frontier.

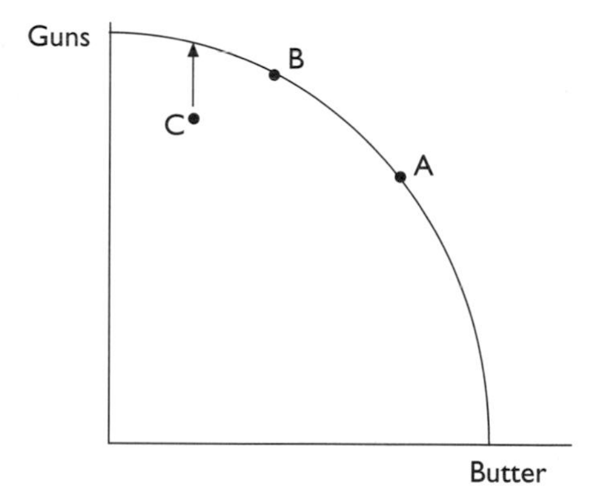

Figure 2.1 A production possibility frontier

Production possibility frontiers are visited again in Chapter 24.

Summary

The fundamental economic problem is that there are only limited resources to meet unlimited wants. Economic systems have evolved to meet this fundamental problem. Such systems can tend towards either a market system or a command system, but all are to some extent mixed.

Opportunity cost is the opportunity you give up in order to make the best choice, while production possibility frontiers show that choices have to be made about how resources are used.

chapter 2 MAKES YOU THINK!

1 Make a list of as many free goods as you can think of. Are they really free in the economics sense?
2 What was the opportunity cost to you of this textbook – i.e. what, if anything, did you give up to get this book?
3 Draw a production possibility frontier for two goods: cheese and yoghurt. Show on your diagram how increases in yoghurt production will affect cheese production if all available resources are being used.

Chapter 3

Specialisation

Before the Industrial Revolution, the vast majority of people worked on the land. They grew food and sometimes grouped together to build shelters. Perhaps some of them made clothes. Some people, on the other hand, lived in the towns where they sold things to other people in the town. Gradually, more *specialist* jobs were needed. For example, advances in medicine meant that doctors were now needed, whilst other people specialised in giving advice on law, and others became priests, and so on. These people, who did not have time to grow their own food, instead now earned money which they *swapped* for the food they needed. In turn, the people who earned this money swapped it for other things which they themselves did not have time to produce because, like most people at that time, they were too busy growing food. This pattern continued until the eighteenth and nineteenth century when the Industrial Revolution led to large numbers of people being needed to work in the factories. Just before this, advances in farming (the Agricultural Revolution) had meant that less people were needed to work on the land. In the course of 100 years, many European countries changed from an economy that had existed since people first settled – i.e. where most people worked in agriculture – to an economy where most people lived in towns and made things.

In economics, production that involves dealing with *raw materials* is called **primary production**; examples are farming, fishing and mining. Production that *manufactures* something from those raw materials is called **secondary production**. And the production of a *service* – such as being a teacher, an accountant, a nurse or a shop worker – is called **tertiary production**. During the second half of the twentieth century, manufacturing industry has been in decline whilst the service sector, on the other hand, has seen increases in employment, in many Western countries. Nowadays in the UK, for example, only 2% of the workforce is employed in agriculture. This sector produces enough to feed everyone else, which leaves most workers free to provide services for one another. The key here is *money*. People do not have to grow their own food, or produce their own car, because everyone is willing to accept money. Everyone is willing to swap what they produce for money, because they are confident that everyone else is willing to do the same. The only question then is: for how much? We will look at that question in later chapters.

Imagine you are alone on a desert island. You would have to do everything for yourself. You might try growing crops, fishing, building a hut etc. But what would you do if you were washed up with a companion? What then would be the best way of surviving? You would probably decide first what needed doing and then what each of you is best at. Then, each of you would spend your time concentrating on what you were best at. This is called **specialisation**, and it can happen between individuals, between regions or between countries. For example, within the UK, the Northamptonshire area and Kettering in particular is famous for shoe production, whilst New Zealand is well known for sheep.

Specialisation between individuals is called **division of labour**. Although this has been a feature of industrial production since before the Industrial Revolution, it really developed and reached a peak of efficiency in the car factories owned by Henry Ford. Therefore, it is sometimes also known as **Fordism**.

One man draws out the wire, another straightens it, a third cuts it, a fourth points, a fifth grinds it at the top for receiving the head; to make the head requires two or three distinct operations; to put it on is a peculiar business, to whiten the pins is another; it is even a trade by itself to put them into the paper.

(Adam Smith describing the making of a pin in his book An Enquiry Into the Nature and Causes of the Wealth of Nations, 1776)

There are two types of division of labour:

1 *Division of labour by product.* This simply means that people specialise in completely separate jobs, making separate goods or services (products). For example, some people make chairs and some make pictures, while others are teachers, lawyers etc.

2 *Division of labour by process.* This is real Fordism where jobs such as making cars are split into a number of processes in which various people specialise. The **mass production** of motor cars is a good example, because the car starts off as sheets of metal and passes through various stages in which different teams of workers put the engine in, install seats, ensure the car is painted, and so on.

Division of labour increases productivity by:

- enabling workers to gain skills in a limited range of tasks
- making it worth the expense of providing specialist tools which will not be left idle for much of the day
- saving time, because workers are not continually changing task and moving from place to place
- allowing workers to specialise in those tasks for which they are best suited

However, the division of labour can also have a number of disadvantages. One of the main ones is the problem of boredom. If a worker is doing one simple task all day, they are unlikely to maintain concentration. Mistakes then occur which result in faulty products. Furthermore, the switch to mass production has led to a loss of skills and craftsmanship – compare a car worker at Rolls Royce with one at General Motors.

If people's skills are very specialised in a particular occupation and that occupation then disappears (e.g. coal-mining in many parts of Western Europe), the person could be unemployed for a very long time. Finally, the division-of-labour principle has resulted in an economic system where each of us is dependent on many other people for our well-being. We rely on farmers for our food, but they in turn rely on manufacturers to provide the equipment needed to produce the food, and the manufacturers in turn rely on people who supply the raw materials, and so on. Economists use the word 'interdependence' to describe this. As we are all 'interdependent', small groups of workers can exert great power. (What would be the result of an electricity power workers' strike?)

Summary

Our economic system is a result of people specialising in different roles. Division of labour takes place by *process* and by *product*. The advantages of division of labour include: increased skill in particular tasks, the saving of time, and machines that are not left idle; whilst the disadvantages include: boredom leading to mistakes, and non-transferable specialist skills leading to areas of high unemployment when those skills are no longer needed.

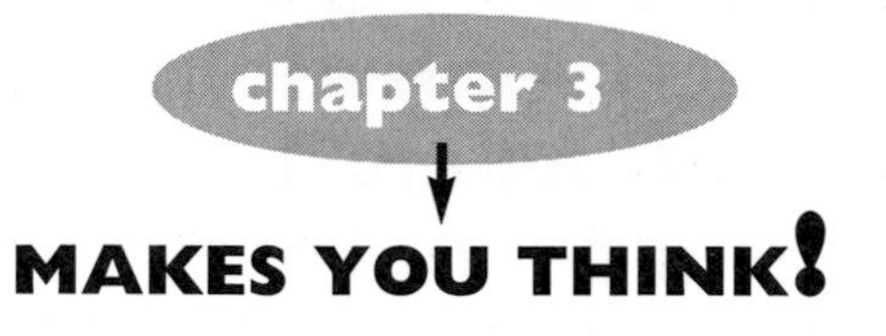

1 Try to list all the effects of a strike by electricity power workers on the rest of the economy.
2 Decide whether each of the following jobs is part of the primary, secondary or tertiary sectors:

   (a) coal-miner
   (b) bank clerk
   (c) car-assembly-line worker
   (d) church minister
   (e) medical doctor.

Figure 3.1 The Renault Megane production line

3 (a) With the help of the photograph, explain what is meant by specialisation.
   (b) For workers on this production line, what might be some of the disadvantages of the division of labour?

Chapter 4

Demand

Markets

In this chapter, we are going to study the fundamental structure of the market economy. A **market** exists wherever there are buyers and sellers of a good. In the past, these buyers and sellers would come together to trade at a particular place on a particular day of the week, and so in each area, the chief town would be the market town, and one day each week would be market day. In the twentieth century, easy travel and communication has led to markets operating without a specific time or place. Markets can take place in corner shops or superstores, or in newspapers and magazines. If someone has something to sell and there is someone to buy it, a market exists and a price will be agreed.

You may have visited markets where it is accepted practice to haggle over the price. The seller sets a high price, and the buyer offers a low price. The seller comes down a bit, and the buyer goes up a bit until they compromise on a price in between the two original offers. While this is the accepted practice in some countries, in others it is not considered appropriate. When buying a house, however, it *is* common to set a high price and then be given lower offers; and in some countries such as the UK, new cars are rarely sold at the list price after negotiation.

The meaning of demand

Now it's bleak house for all as chill wind turns to an ill wind

The housing market took a further battering this week with the disclosure that nine out of ten mortgage borrowers who lose their job or fall ill will face repossession if the Government presses ahead with plans to restrict mortgage benefit.

But the house buying public has already reached the conclusion contained in damning research from the Department of the Environment. In place of the normal spring house buying fever the property market is suffering with hypothermia brought on by the chill winds of unemployment and Government policy.

Building society lending figures ... confirm that this year's buying season – such as it was – is over. Mortgage demand last month fell by nearly £1 billion ...

(The Guardian, 20 May 1995)

When the economy is prospering and people have extra money to spend, they will be prepared to offer more for the house that they desire. The house will then be sold to the person who is willing to offer the most money. When unemployment is high, or people have little spare money because taxes are high or interest rates make loan repayments expensive, people will offer *less* than the asking price in the expectation that fewer people will be able to afford to buy houses. They assume that the seller will settle for a lower price because there is little demand for houses since people are finding it difficult to afford the prices being asked.

- If you have a house to sell, would you prefer a high price or a low price?
- If you were buying a house, would you prefer a high price or a low price?

By answering these simple questions, you have worked out the theory of **demand**. Now we will make it a little more formal.

The demand curve

Generally, people will buy more of something the cheaper it is. That is why shops have 'sales': if they reduce the price, more will be bought. Economists often find it useful to show this simple idea on a diagram. First we construct a table (a **demand schedule**) to show the amount of a product that people are prepared to buy at a particular price – see Table 4.1 which shows the numbers of crisp packets that can be sold by a company at given prices. We then plot this information on a graph – see Figure 4.1. *Note that the price always goes up the side while the quantity always goes along the bottom.* A **demand curve** (which may be a straight line, but is still then called a curve) shows the amounts of a product that would be bought at a particular price as long as everything else stays the same. When the price changes, there is a movement *along* the demand curve. For example, if the price falls from 30p a packet to 20p, there will be a move from point A to point B. Similarly, if there is a price rise from 30p to 40p, there will be a movement along the demand curve from point A to C.

Table 4.1 A demand schedule

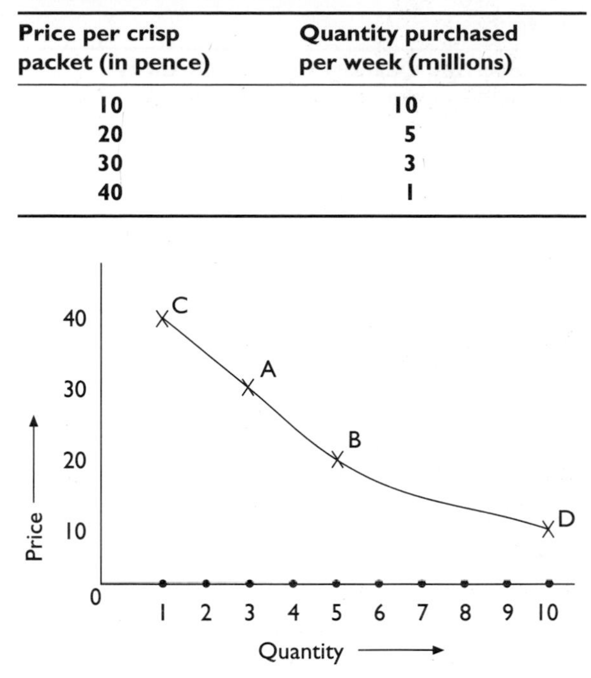

Price per crisp packet (in pence)	Quantity purchased per week (millions)
10	10
20	5
30	3
40	1

Figure 4.1 A demand curve

Shifts in the demand curve

Income

It is important to remember that the demand curve shows the relationship between quantity and price when everything else that may affect spending decisions stays the same. But in the real world, things rarely stay the same. One of the major influences on how much of something people will buy is their **income**: if people have more money to spend, they are likely to buy more of any product. Take for example the demand schedule shown in Table 4.2. Draw two demand curves, on one and the same diagram, showing the information in the table. What happens to your demand curve as income rises from £150 to £300 a week? Answer: generally, as income rises, the demand curve *shifts to the right*. On the other hand, a fall in your disposable income (i.e. in what you actually have to spend) will result in a *shift to the left* by the demand curve.

Table 4.2 A demand schedule for two different levels of income

Price of crisps (in pence)	Quantity demanded where income = £150 a week	Quantity demanded where income = £300 a week
10	5	7
20	4	6
30	2	5
40	0	4

Complements and substitutes

If the price of burgers at a fast-food outlet rises, then although the price of *chips* remains the same, people may now buy *fewer* chips. This is because they are now buying fewer burgers as a result of the price rise, and because of this they will not want the chips that normally go with them. Economists would say that burger and chips are **complements**. Other goods, on the other hand, may be **substitutes** for one another (i.e. good alternatives). For example, in the spring of 1996, worry about the health risks associated with BSE in beef led to people switching to buying lamb instead. Demand for lamb increased as a result of something happening to beef.

Advertising

In how many ways does the advert shown in Figure 4.2 try to convince the reader to buy the car? The purpose of advertising is to encourage people to buy more of a good or service than they would otherwise have bought. Advertisements can try to persuade you that the product is better than a rival, or they can merely give information and so alert you to the existence of the product. Either way, if the advertising is successful, more of the product will be bought at the existing price, and so the demand curve will shift to the right.

Fashion and taste

Changes in fashion and taste can lead to shifts in the demand curve. Styles of dress (e.g. miniskirts or flared trousers) have been 'in' or 'out' at various times. When styles are 'in', the demand curve will shift to the right. When they are 'out', it will shift to the left.

Legislation

Changes in the law can also affect demand. For example, if the government of a country with strict gun control were now to approve of people owning their own guns, then the demand curve for guns would be likely to shift to the right.

Population

Finally, changes in the size or the composition of the population will affect demand. If the size of the population declines, then demand curves will move to the left, whilst a rise in the population results in shifts to the right in demand curves. However, this case is not very helpful, because increases or decreases in the population tend to take place over a very long period of time, and many other changes – such as in income levels – also take place during that time. A change in the make-up of the population may be more useful to consider. For example, a sudden increase in the birth rate will lead to a shift in the demand curve for prams and pushchairs.

Throughout the Western world, there is a growing proportion of the population who are over 65. How do you think this will affect demand?

Exceptions

Inferior goods

The demand for most goods behaves in the way that has been described, and such goods are called **normal goods**. However, there are some

CLUB MED OR OASIS.
HOW WILL NICOLE DECIDE?

Nicole is in a dilemma. Two stunning models are waiting beneath her balcony - and she has to choose one of them.

It won't be easy. After all, both the Clio Oasis and Clio Club Med special editions share the refined contours of the new style Clio.

Both have tinted glass, a tilt-and-slide sunroof and a stereo radio/cassette with detachable fascia. And both offer a choice of 3 or 5 door versions. What's more, thanks to an all-new 1.2 litre 60 bhp D.I.E.T. engine and a 5-speed gearbox, Nicole will love driving either car. (Thanks to a computer padlock engine immobiliser, no-one else will get the chance.)

Papa is no help. Now he knows both models have front seat belt pretensioners, side impact protection and driver's airbag (optional on the Oasis), he's happy whatever his daughter decides.

They can't be split on value either. Both cost astonishingly little for their equipment levels, with Oasis prices starting at just **£7,695** on the road.

No, Nicole will just have to find another way of deciding. Any ideas?

For more information on the Clio Oasis and Clio Club Med, call free on 0800 52 51 50.

RENAULT
CARS
WITH FLAIR

TYPICAL EXAMPLE	8.9% APR	£89 deposit*	
		CLIO OASIS 1.2 3dr	CLIO CLUB MED 1.2 3dr
Cash Price inc. on the road costs†		£7695.00	£8,805.00
Deposit		£89.00	£89.00
Monthly Repayments		£185.71 x48	£212.82 x48
Total Credit Price		£9,103.08**	£10,404.36**

FROM £89 DEPOSIT & FREE INSURANCE‡

RENAULT recommend elf

Figure 4.2 A press advert for the Renault Clio Club Med and Oasis

exceptions. Some goods are bought by people as a cheaper substitute for what they really want. If their income were to rise, then, rather than buy more of the cheaper good, they may buy something else instead. So, although we would expect a rise in income to lead to an increase in demand for such cheaper goods, there is actually a *fall* instead. These types of good are called **inferior goods**. Unfortunately, inferior goods tend to be just that: in particular, inferior in terms of what is best for health. On the other hand, an increase in income may cause problems for the environment. For example, in a supermarket, white bread tends to be very cheap – in 1996, a loaf of white bread could be bought from major British supermarket chains for 29p – whereas healthier wholemeal bread can cost two or three times as much. Fresh fruit and vegetables are also expensive when compared with packaged food which contains lots of fat, sugar and salt. However, as people's incomes rise, although they may now switch to healthier food, they may also switch from using public transport to using their own car and so increase pollution.

Status goods

Some goods are bought purely because they are expensive. Diamonds and rare metals have traditionally been an example, but these days man-made objects can also take on a desirability due to their expense. What about a Rolls-Royce, a Porsche or a BMW? In fact, BMW is a particularly good example. This company used to produce fairly ordinary mid-priced motor cars. Then, they adopted a strange marketing strategy to sell more cars. Rather than reduce the price to increase sales, they decided to do the opposite. They decided to put the price up, but not by a small amount. They increased the price dramatically, making a BMW something that was out of the reach of many car buyers, and therefore something that people would aspire to. It worked, but only because BMW make extremely good cars. The high price was an effective way of alerting people to that fact. Thus, **status goods** (or **ostentatious goods** as they are also often known) have a demand curve that goes in the opposite way to most goods – see Figure 4.3.

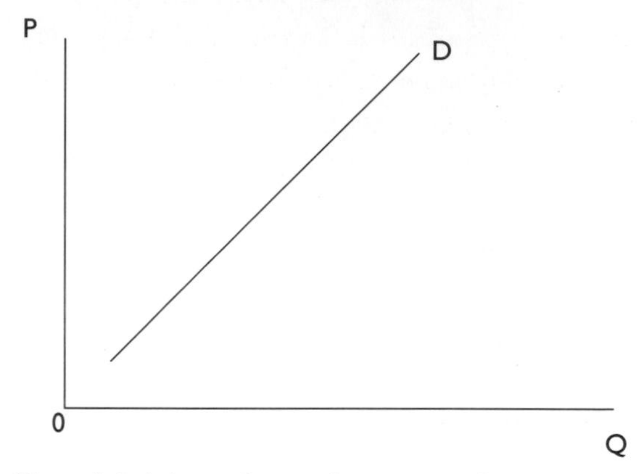

Figure 4.3 A demand curve for status goods

Individual and market demand

There are two types of demand curve. We can draw one reflecting an *individual's* spending decisions, but we can also add up all the individual spending decisions to show how *overall* demand for a particular product will change. This latter curve is called the **market demand curve**, and it is most useful for firms: an accurate market demand curve would enable a firm to predict by how much their sales would fall given a price increase. In reality, however, this is something they don't know: they can really only make a guess and see what happens.

Summary

The laws of demand are:

- The higher the price, the less will be the quantity demanded

- The lower the price, the greater will be the quantity demanded

Changes in the price of a good or service will result in a change in the quantity demanded, and this is shown by a movement along the demand curve.

Changes in anything *other* than the price of the product will result in a shift to the right or the left by the demand curve. These shifts can be brought about by changes in:

- income
- fashion or taste
- advertising
- the population
- legislation
- changes in the price of other goods

There are exceptions to the general laws of demand: inferior goods and status goods.

The market demand curve is found by combining all the individual demand curves.

chapter 4

MAKES YOU THINK!

1 Make two lists. One should contain as many pairs of complements as you can think of, whilst the other should contain as many pairs of substitutes as you can come up with.

2 Draw a demand curve for new cars which starts high on the left and slopes downwards to the right. Suppose the government cuts taxes, leaving people with more of their income to spend. Show how the demand curve for new cars might move.

3 Between 1973 and 1975, the price of oil quadrupled. Explain, using demand diagrams, the effect you would expect this to have on each of the following:

(a) petrol
(b) gas-powered central-heating systems
(c) plastic toys.

Chapter 5

Supply

The meaning of supply

When Henry Ford introduced mass production to the car industry in the 1920s, he opened the way for huge reductions in the costs of production by benefiting from division of labour. Similarly, microtechnology has led to cheaper computers and calculators. On the other hand, for most goods and services, costs tend to rise each year, leading in turn to steady *price* rises. However, some products, such as agricultural products, have prices that can go up or down each year, depending on how successful the harvest has been.

Supply is the quantity of something that sellers are prepared to sell at a particular price.

The supply curve

Whereas consumers prefer low prices, producers prefer high prices. Think about it. If you have something to sell, you will try to get for it the highest price possible. In fact, the more you can get for something, the more likely you are to be tempted to sell it. This is illustrated in the **supply curve** – see Figure 5.1. A fall in price will lead to a fall in the quantity supplied. This is shown by a movement along the supply curve from point A to point B – a *contraction* in supply. Similarly, a rise in price will result in a rise in the quantity supplied – an *extension* of supply. Thus, just as with the demand curve, a change in price will result in a movement *along* the supply curve.

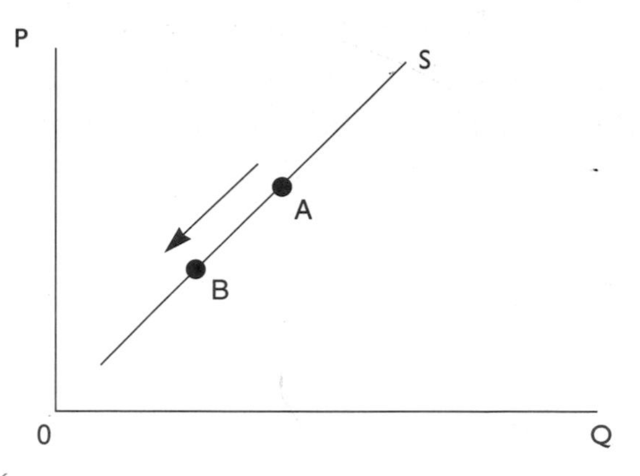

Figure 5.1 A supply curve

If someone wants to buy something that you own, you may be reluctant to sell. However, the higher the price that you are offered, the more tempted you will be to sell. Similarly, suppose you owned some land, and you realised that your neighbour had started selling water from a well. If your neighbour received 5 pence a bottle, you may not do anything. But if your neighbour starts receiving 50 pence for each bottle, you may decide that it is time to give up your job and look for your own water to sell. In Western Europe, the sale of bottled mineral water (from numerous sources) has mushroomed as new suppliers have entered the market, tempted by premium prices.

Shifts in the supply curve

As with the demand curve, various things can happen to make the supply curve shift to the left or the right. A shift to the left illustrates a *decrease* in supply, whilst a shift to the right illustrates an *increase* in supply. A number of factors can cause shifts in the supply curve:

Costs of production

An increase in the **costs of production** will cause the supply curve to shift to the left, because producers will now be willing to supply the same quantity only at a higher price. Similarly, a reduction in production costs will result in a shift to the right. Production costs include the cost of raw materials, labour costs (wages), taxes and rent.

In the spring of 1995, German engineering workers went on strike to try to achieve a reduction in their weekly working hours to 35 hours per week. The effect of such a reduction in working hours could be shown as a shift to the left in the supply curve for engineering products, since the costs of production would increase.

Technology

New technology used in the production process can lead to a shift to the right in the supply curve, as the same quantity can now be produced at a lower cost. Many things which were once very expensive are now relatively cheaper. The adoption by Henry Ford of mass-production techniques allowed the price of cars to fall so that ordinary families could afford one. Something similar has happened to computers during the 1980s and 1990s. A 486 personal computer is more powerful than the sort of machine that only large companies could afford in 1980.

Taxation

An increase in the tax on a product will make any quantity of that product more expensive. Therefore, the effect of a new tax or of an increase in a current tax will be shown as a shift to the left in the supply curve.

In the November 1994 Budget, the British Chancellor of the Exchequer (i.e. the finance minister) Kenneth Clarke planned to increase the value-added tax (VAT) charged on household gas and electricity. This decision was overturned by Parliament, and he was forced to raise the money by an alternative approach. He decided to raise the money by increasing the tax on alcohol, tobacco and petrol. An increase in the tax on petrol affects not only the supply curve for petrol but also the supply curve for those other products which are affected by the price of petrol: these will also move to the left.

The weather

The weather plays a critical role in the supply of agricultural goods. Bad weather can devastate a crop, leading to much less being supplied at any price (i.e. to a shift to the left in the supply curve). On the other hand, good weather can lead to a bumper harvest which should lead to falls in price as farmers are desperate to sell their crops. (For an account of why in European Union countries this doesn't happen, see Chapter 19.) Thus, bad weather can shift the supply curve to the left, whilst good weather can shift it to the right – see Figure 5.2. In this way, a drought in Costa Rica can affect the supply of coffee in European supermarkets.

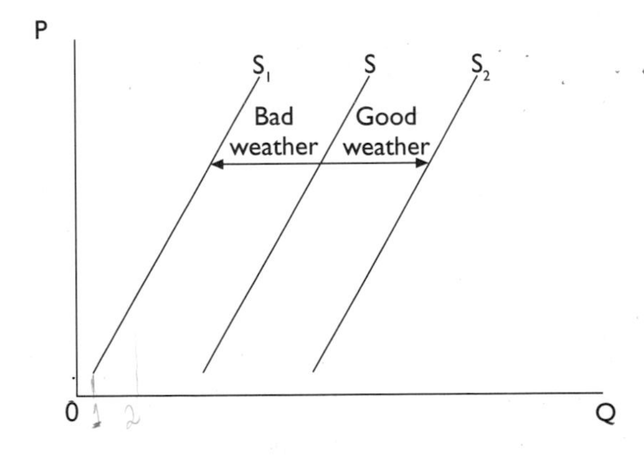

Figure 5.2 How the weather affects the supply curve for agricultural products

Joint supply

Some goods are in **joint supply** with other goods. For example, when cows are killed for beef, their skins are used to produce leather. Therefore, if the price of beef were to rise, farmers might supply more beef, and by doing so they will make available more leather, even though the price of leather has itself not risen.

Summary

The higher the price, the greater will be the quantity supplied; and the lower the price, the less will be the quantity supplied. The supply curve can shift to the left or the right, and this is caused by changes in:

- production costs
- technology
- taxation
- the weather
- the price of related goods

chapter 5

MAKES YOU THINK!

1 In the spring of 1995, German engineering workers went on strike to try to achieve a reduction in their weekly working hours to 35 hours per week. Show how a reduction in working hours would affect the supply curve for engineering products.

2 In the November-1994 Budget, the Chancellor of the Exchequer Kenneth Clarke planned to increase the value-added tax (VAT) charged on household gas and electricity. The decision was overturned by Parliament, and he was forced to raise the money by an alternative approach. He decided to raise the money by increasing the tax on alcohol, tobacco and petrol.

Show how an increase in the tax on petrol affects not only the supply curve for petrol but also the supply curve for other products which are affected by the price of petrol.

3 Show, by using supply curves, how a drought in Costa Rica can affect the supply, and therefore the price, of coffee in British supermarkets.

Chapter 6

Price

During the 1980s, there was a constant rise in the price of houses in the UK, with a very rapid rise between 1988 and 1990. The demand for housing was exceeding the number of houses for sale, and the way to decide who would get a house when several people wanted it was to put the price up until only one of the potential buyers was willing to pay the asking price. During the early 1990s, however, the average price of houses fell. For various reasons (mainly to do with people having less money to spend – i.e. a fall in incomes), people were less keen on buying houses, and sellers this time responded by *dropping* prices until somebody was willing to pay the asking price.

We shall see during this chapter that **price** is the result of a *negotiation* between buyers and sellers. In housing, there is a clear and obvious negotiation between one seller and a few prospective purchasers. The process is less obvious, however, when dealing with chocolate bars or washing liquid. However, the principle is the same.

Commodities enjoyed a terrific year with prices of base metals such as copper and aluminium soaring in response to renewed demand. Oil started the year almost comatose with Brent crude prices dipping below $13 per barrel. It rallied steadily, reaching $18-plus in the summer because of strengthening demand and falling inventories, but since then has fallen back, leaving most oil companies averaging prices of $15–16 for the year.

News in November that Opec was maintaining 24.5 million barrels per day did little for the oil price. The problem is that increased demand from economic recovery in the US has largely been satisfied by non-Opec supplies which continue to rise. Some 800,000 of the 1 million barrel increase in demand for oil in 1994 came from non-Opec producers such as the North Sea and that pattern could well repeat itself in 1995.

(The Times, 30 December 1994)

The meaning of the equilibrium price

We now need to remember what we have learnt in the chapters on demand and supply. The demand curve shows all the quantities that consumers are willing to buy at different prices. The supply curve shows all the quantities that producers are willing to sell at different prices. The assumptions here are that consumers will demand a greater quantity as price falls, and that producers will supply a greater quantity as price rises. If we draw both the demand curve and the supply curve on the same diagram, we will get Figure 6.1. Notice that there is only one place where the amount that consumers are willing to buy at a particular price is the same as the amount that producers are willing to sell at that price: it is the point where the demand curve and the supply curve converge on the same combination of price and quantity – in other words, the point where they cross. This point is called the **equilibrium price**. This is the price that will be settled on. Let's think about why this is the case.

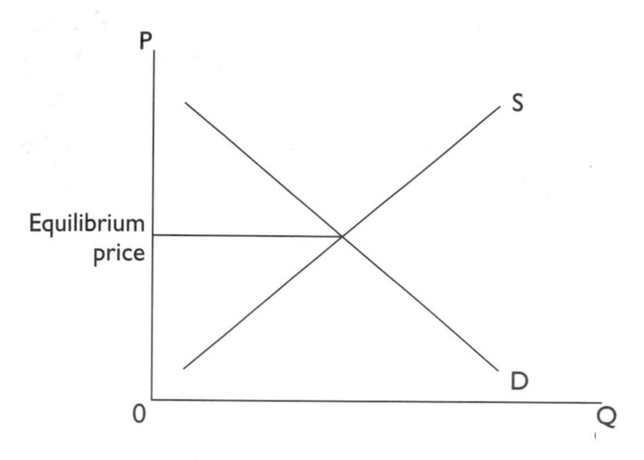

Figure 6.1 The equilibrium price is where the demand and supply curves cross

Suppose a producer of potato crisps is willing to supply the following quantities at the following prices, and consumers are willing to buy the following quantities at these prices:

Price (pence)	Quantity demanded (million bags per month)	Quantity supplied (million bags per month)
22	6	1
24	5	2
26	3	3
28	2	4
30	1	6

If a price of 22 pence is charged, then, in search of a bargain, consumers would like to buy 6 million bags of crisps. However, at that price it is not worth the producer's while to supply more than 1 million bags of crisps. There will thus be a shortage of crisps, and shops will report to the manufacturer that they could sell many more crisps. The producers could then respond by producing more crisps, but the supply schedule shows us that they are not prepared to supply more at that price. They will therefore increase the price instead. If a price of 30 pence is now charged, consumers will only be prepared to buy 1 million bags of crisps. Producers, however, would be happily supplying 6 million bags of crisps. There would therefore be a glut of crisps, with unopened boxes not being sold. In this case, producers would have to cut the price, and at the same time they would cut back on production. Eventually, by trial and error, a price will be arrived at where all the crisps that are supplied are bought and where there is no overproduction and no shortages. The market is now in *equilibrium.*

Another name for the equilibrium price is the **market clearing price**: all the crisps are bought or 'cleared' from the market, and nobody who is willing to pay that price goes without. In the example shown in the table below, the equilibrium price is £75 because at that price demand is equal to supply. £75 is thus the market clearing price. At a price of £100, there would be an oversupply or a surplus, while at a price of £50 there would be a shortage or excess demand.

Price (£)	Quantity demanded	Quantity supplied
100	75	1,000
75	100	100
50	500	50

The effects of changes in demand and supply

In the chapters on demand and supply, we saw that many things can cause the demand and supply curves to shift to the left or the right. A particular price only remains as the equilibrium price as long as nothing happens to make the demand or supply curve shift. Economists – as already mentioned – emphasise this idea by using the phrase 'all other things remaining equal' – or, if they're being pedantic, the Latin phrase *ceteris paribus* which means the same thing.

So what happens if there is an increase in demand? Figure 6.2 shows the demand curve shifting to the right to reflect the increase in demand: demand curve D becomes D_1 and now crosses the supply curve at a higher point. Therefore, there is now a higher equilibrium price (P_2) and a greater quantity demanded (Q_2).

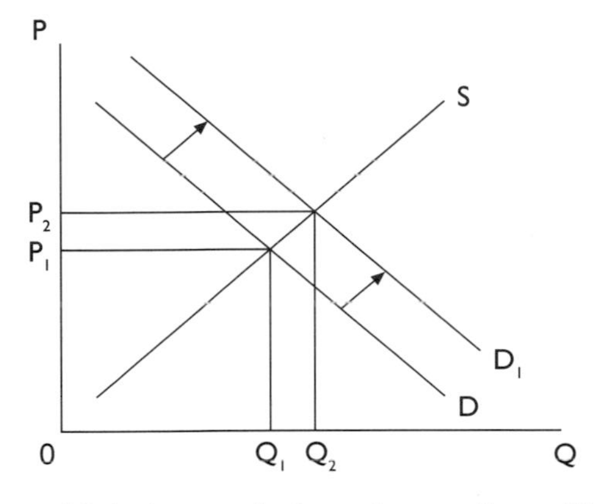

Figure 6.2 An increase in demand causes the equilibrium price to go up

A decrease in demand, on the other hand, causes the demand curve to shift to the left, as in Figure 6.3. The demand curve (D_1) now crosses

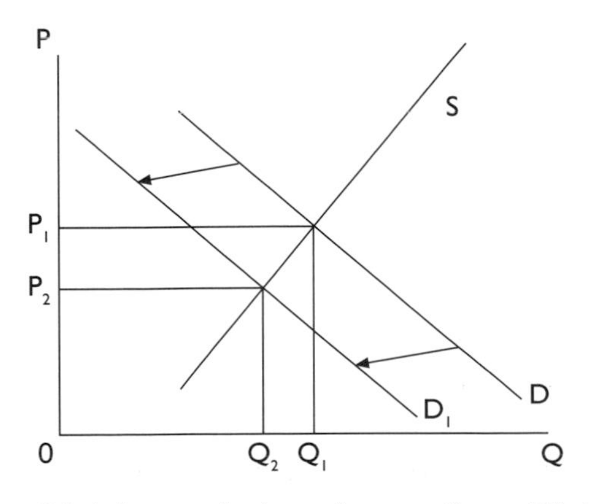

Figure 6.3 A decrease in demand causes the equilibrium price to go down

the supply curve at a lower point, with a lower equilibrium price (P_2) and a smaller quantity demanded (Q_2).

What about the effects of changes in supply? An increase in supply will shift the supply curve to the right, whilst a decrease in supply will shift it to the left. When the supply curves shifts to the left, it crosses the demand curve at a higher point. Therefore, the equilibrium price will be higher and the quantity demanded will be lower – see Figure 6.4. A shift to the right in the supply curve will lead to more being demanded at a lower price.

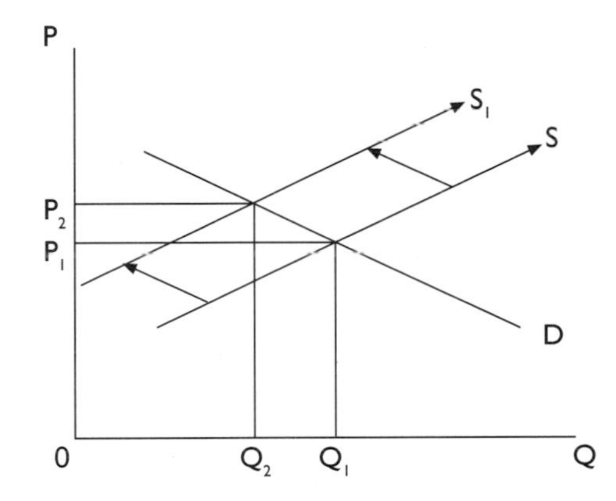

Figure 6.4 A decrease in supply causes the equilibrium price to go up

Consumer sovereignty

The producer can set any price they like, but the consumer can still *choose* whether or not to buy. If there are lots of substitutes, then the consumer can always buy from another producer. Sometimes, there will be very little choice because there is only one producer (for example, the consumer has very little choice about where to get their electricity). However, the consumer can still choose to buy *less* of that product if the price is too high (although yes, I know that a certain amount *is* considered a necessity). Thus, the consumer has the final say: the consumer is 'sovereign'.

So what determines the price of a bread roll? If you were to ask 10 people this question, they would probably give you a list including flour and yeast (i.e. the raw materials), workers' wages, electricity etc. This is all perfectly correct, but it is a description only of the costs of production, i.e. of the things that affect *supply*. As students of economics, we know that this is only half the story: we must not forget that, no matter what the producer wants to charge, the price has to reflect what consumers are willing to pay. To put it more formally, the price of a bread roll is determined by both supply and demand.

Summary

The equilibrium price is also known as the market clearing price, and it is the point where the demand and the supply curves cross.

The equilibrium price will rise and more will be bought if there is an increase in demand. The equilibrium price will fall and less will be bought if there is a decrease in demand. The equilibrium price will rise and less will be bought if there is a decrease in supply. The equilibrium price will fall and more will be bought if there is an increase in supply.

A shortage occurs when the selling price is below the equilibrium price. If the price charged is above the equilibrium price, there will be a glut (over-supply). The equilibrium or market clearing price is where the producers can sell all that they are willing to produce at a particular price, and where the consumers can buy all that they are willing to buy at that price.

Price is determined by the interaction of demand and supply.

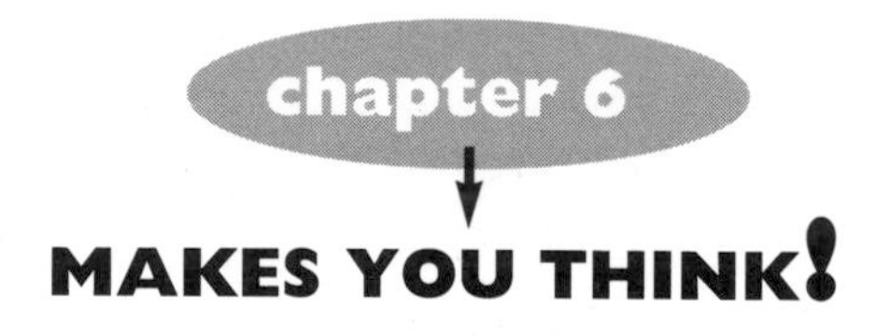

1 Explain, using demand and supply curves, why shops have sales periods.
2 Suppose you were arranging a concert. What things would you have to take into account when deciding on a ticket price?
3 (a) If, after the concert, you had lots of unsold tickets, would this make you less likely to arrange another?
  (b) If you quickly ran out of tickets, how might this affect your pricing of your next event?

Chapter 7

Elasticity

The story of oil

For many years until the early 1970s, oil was a very cheap fuel. In the early 1970s, petrol in Western Europe was sold at around 7 pence per litre. Within 20 years, however, the price of petrol had increased by about 50 pence per litre. Things started to change in 1973 when the Yom Kippur war between Egypt/Syria and Israel broke out. Although Israel won the war, the Arab oil-producing countries found that by cutting back on oil production they could force up the price and make life very uncomfortable for industrialised countries. This was because, since oil was so cheap, it was relied on as a very heavily used source of power, not just for petrol but for electricity too. Between 1973 and 1974, the price of oil rose from $3 a barrel to $12. As a result of this quadrupling in price, the demand for oil fell. Countries developed power stations using alternative fuels, such as coal-fired and nuclear power stations; and car manufacturers started to produce cars that were much more 'fuel efficient' than any that had been made before.

However, although the reactions to the price increase were very major and profound, they took many years to come about: in the short term, power stations still needed oil until new ones could be built; and cars could still manage only 5 km per litre until they could be replaced. So, in the year after the 300% price rise, the quantity demanded fell by only 5%. In the short term, the demand for oil was thus very **inelastic**. In the long term, however, it was very **elastic**. The terms elastic and inelastic will be more fully explained in this chapter, but inelastic basically means: not responsive to changes in price; and elastic means: responsive to changes in price.

The meaning of elasticity

Elasticity is one of those ideas in economics that can seem complicated, but really the idea is very simple. It is also a very important idea for businesses and governments. We have seen in previous chapters that as the price rises people will tend to buy less. If you think about it, this must be true. People's income is limited, and so if the price of everything they buy goes up, there is no way they will be able to afford everything that they bought before. They must therefore cut back, but will they cut back on everything by the same amount? The answer is probably no! Some things are more important than others, and some things have cheaper substitutes. Just by *how much* demand for a product changes when there is a change in either price or a person's income is called elasticity.

Types of elasticity

The amount of anything that people will buy can change for a number of reasons, and each one of these gives rise to a particular kind of elasticity. In theory, the exact elasticity can be worked out if we know exactly what has happened to bring about a change in the amount bought.

Price elasticity of demand

The **price elasticity of demand** shows how much less of something people will buy if the price goes up. It is worked out by applying this formula:

$$\frac{\textbf{percentage change in quantity demanded}}{\textbf{percentage change in price}}$$

So, suppose the price of a Big Mac is $2.00 and you buy 10 Big Macs each month. Then suppose that there is a price rise to $2.20 and that as a result you now only buy 7 Big Macs each month. Let's use the above formula to work out the price elasticity of demand:

1 Percentage change in quantity demanded: you did buy 10, but now you buy only 7, so the change amounts to 3. A change of 3 out of 10 is 30%, so the percentage change in quantity demanded here is 30% – or more correctly, −30% to show that it is 30% *less* rather than more.
2 Percentage change in price: you used to pay $2.00, but the price has now increased to $2.20. That is a 10% price increase.

$$\frac{-30\%}{+10\%} = -3$$

The price elasticity of demand is therefore −3. However, we expect the quantity demanded to go down when the price goes up, and indeed the quantity demanded to go up when the price goes down, and for this reason we would expect the answer to be a *negative*, i.e. '−'. We would therefore only bother to use a sign if the answer were unexpected – i.e. where a '+' occurs instead. This would happen if, when the price rose, the quantity demanded rose as well – as in the case of an 'ostentatious good' (remember the BMW in Chapter 4?).

The question for any business when deciding on a price increase is: will it make more money by putting up its prices? The answer lies in the elasticity factor. If a 10% increase in price is going to result in a 30% fall in the quantity demanded, then the business is going to receive less revenue, the number that comes out of the formula is greater than one, and economists describe demand as *elastic*. However, what about the following situation?

You like Big Macs so much that the price can rise to $2.50 and you will still only cut your consumption from 10 each month to 9. Let's use the formula again and see what comes out:

$$\frac{\textbf{percentage change in quantity demanded}}{\textbf{percentage change in price}} = \frac{-10}{+25}$$

$$= 0.4$$

The price elasticity of demand is now *less* than 1 – i.e. 0.4 – and this means that McDonalds could safely raise its prices knowing that its revenue would also rise.

In exceptional circumstances, the price of a hamburger might rise by 10%, and this might lead to 10% fewer hamburgers being bought. In this case, the elasticity would be exactly 1. This has a special name, an **elasticity of unity**, and it means that the firm's revenue will stay exactly the same.

Note that throughout this section we have assumed that your own reaction to price changes is the same as everyone else's reaction, but this is probably not going to be the case. Of course, it is how *all* potential customers respond to a price change that decides just how a firm's revenue will change.

The government and price elasticity of demand

Price elasticity of demand is an important idea for the government, because when the Chancellor (finance minister) increases a tax in the budget, he plans to increase the government's revenue. However, some taxes are put on things to *discourage* people from buying them. By how much would you advise the Chancellor to increase taxes on petrol and tobacco?

Price elasticity of supply

We have seen in previous chapters that producers will supply more as the price rises, so the question now is 'How much more?' We find the price elasticity of supply by using the formula:

$$\frac{\text{percentage change in quantity supplied}}{\text{percentage change in price}}$$

So if there were a price rise of 10% and producers increased the amount they were prepared to supply by 5%, the price elasticity of supply would be:

$$\frac{\text{percentage change in quantity supplied}}{\text{percentage change in price}} = \frac{5}{10}$$

$$= 0.5$$

This is less than one, and so the price elasticity of supply is here *inelastic*.

Income elasticity of demand

Income elasticity of demand measures how much more (or less) of something people will consume if their income changes. Generally, people will buy more of something if they have a rise in their income, but some things they may already have enough of, and other things may be cut back on as people switch to buying better-quality or healthier products (yes, sadly, the healthiest things are the more expensive, so low income often equals poor health).

Suppose somebody has a pay rise of 5%, and that as a result they buy 10% more fresh fruit. Their income elasticity of demand for fresh fruit will be:

$$\frac{\text{percentage change in quantity demanded}}{\text{percentage change in income}} = \frac{10}{5}$$

$$= 2$$

On the other hand, that same 5% pay rise may result in 10% less cheap white bread being bought as people switch to wholemeal, so that:

$$\frac{\text{percentage change in quantity demanded}}{\text{percentage change in income}} = \frac{-10}{+5}$$

$$= -2$$

A negative income elasticity of demand indicates an 'inferior good' (see Chapter 4): as people's incomes rise, *less* of it is bought.

Cross price elasticity of demand

Cross price elasticity of demand – which sounds very complicated but isn't – measures how much the quantity demanded of something will change when the price of *something else* alters. Come with me to the local fish shop. Unfortunately, over-fishing in the Atlantic has meant that my favourite fish, haddock, has gone up in price. It's now £1 more expensive than cod, which is still at the same price as last month, so I think I'd better have cod instead. Although the price of cod has stayed exactly the same, the quantity of cod demanded will increase because the price of haddock has gone up and because cod and haddock are *substitutes* for one another (see Chapter 4).

The next week we go to the chip shop and find that cod too has risen in price. As a result, we decide that fish and chips are becoming far too expensive, and so we buy a box of chicken from the Kentucky shop instead. This time we are buying less fish because its price has increased, but we are also going without the chips. The price of chips has stayed the same, but the quantity demanded has fallen because they tend to be bought together with fish – i.e. fish and chips are 'complements' or complementary goods (see Chapter 4). Note that in economics, a complementary good is not one that is given for free: it is something that tends to be bought to go with something else. When applying the formula below for cross price elasticity of demand, we find that, given a price rise in *another* product (i.e. a '+' sign is involved), if the quantity demanded of the *original* product we are dealing with also then goes up (i.e. a '+' sign again), then the elasticity will be positive (because a plus divided by a plus will give us a plus); and that shows us that we have a substitute, where more will be bought as a result of the price rise in the other good. On the other hand, if we find that given a rise in the price of another good (i.e. a '+' sign), the quantity demanded of the original good goes down (i.e. a '−' sign), then the elasticity will be negative (because a minus divided by a plus will give us a minus); and that shows us that we have a complement, where less of the other good is bought and so less will be bought of the thing that goes with it.

The formula for cross price elasticity of demand is thus:

$$\frac{\textbf{percentage change in the quantity demanded of good X}}{\textbf{percentage change in the price of good Y}}$$

So, returning to the fish shop, if the price of haddock goes up by 20%, and as a result I buy 50% more cod, then putting the numbers into the formula, we find:

$$\frac{\textbf{percentage change in the quantity demanded of good X}}{\textbf{percentage change in the price of good Y}}$$

$$= \frac{+50}{+20} = +2.5$$

Cod and haddock are substitutes.

However, if I decide to buy 50% fewer chips because the price of fish has gone up by 20%, we find:

$$\frac{\textbf{percentage change in the quantity demanded of good X}}{\textbf{percentage change in the price of good Y}}$$

$$= \frac{-50}{+20} = -2.5$$

Fish and chips are complements.

Elasticity and the demand curve

If the price change were to result in no change at all to the quantity demanded, then we would describe the situation as being *perfectly inelastic* – see Figure 7.1. The opposite theoretical extreme is a *perfectly elastic* demand curve where any change in price will result in *no quantity at all* being demanded – see figure 7.2. The other theoretical special case is where elasticity is exactly 1. Here the percentage change in quantity demanded will be *equal* to the percentage change in price, and revenue will therefore remain unchanged. This – as already mentioned – is **unitary elasticity**, or price elasticity of unity, and the demand curve for this is shown in Figure 7.3.

Summary

Elasticity describes the effect of a change in price or income on the quantity demanded. Elasticity can be measured using the appropriate formula, and it is a useful tool for business and for government in trying to predict how people will react, in their spending patterns, to a decision. However, in reality the elasticity will not be known until the change in price or income has already taken place. On the other hand, previous experience does give a pretty strong clue as to what the elasticity is likely to be.

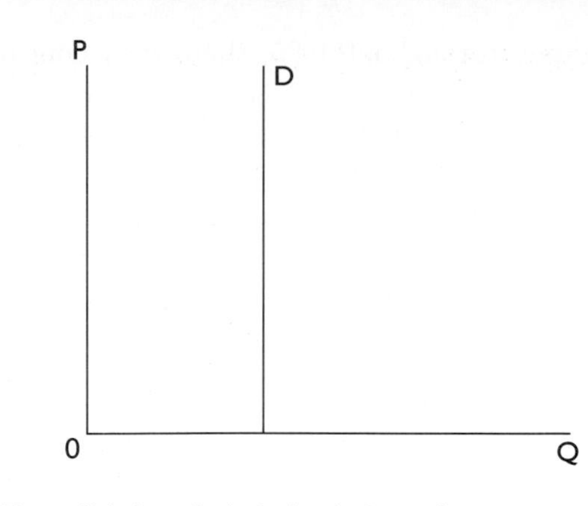

Figure 7.1 A perfectly inelastic demand curve

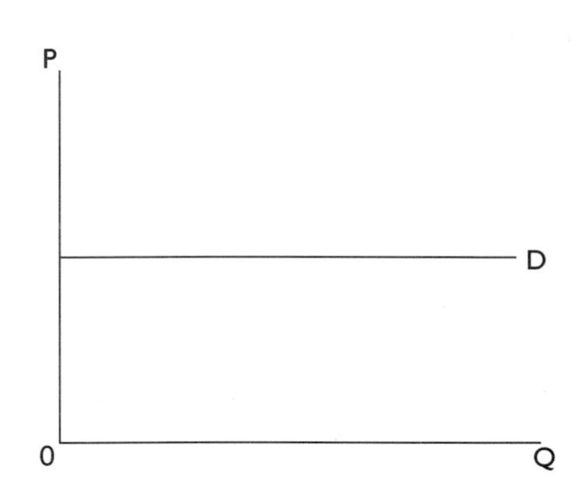

Figure 7.2 A perfectly elastic demand curve

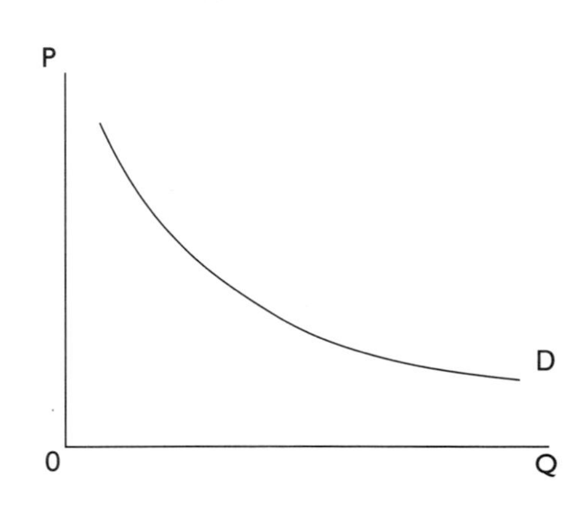

Figure 7.3 A demand curve for unitary elasticity

chapter 7

MAKES YOU THINK!

1 Which of the following pairs of goods would you describe as substitutes, and which as complements:

(a) cheese and biscuits
(b) beef and lamb
(c) suits and ties
(d) apples and pears
(e) pen and paper
(f) CDs and tapes
(g) bacon and eggs
(h) skirt and trousers
(i) Ford Fiesta and Rover 100
(j) a holiday in Tenerife and a holiday in Tenby?

2 What would be the relevant elasticity in the following circumstances?

(a) increase in quantity demanded by 20%, increase in price by 30%
(b) increase in price by 20%, fall in quantity demanded by 10%
(c) increase in income by 10%, increase in quantity demanded by 20%
(d) increase in income by 20%, fall in quantity demanded by 30%
(e) increase in price of good X by 10%, increase in quantity demanded of good Y by 5%.

3 For each of the above examples, decide which type of good or service we are dealing with – i.e. normal, inferior, substitute, complement etc.

Chapter 8

The factors of production

MPs condemn pay rise for gas chief

In an acrimonious clash in the Commons, the Labour leader said the 75 per cent rise for Cedric Brown and the proposed average 16 per cent pay reduction for 2,300 sales assistants were 'offensive to the British sense of justice'.

The Commons clash erupted after it emerged that British Gas is asking for pay cuts of 16 per cent, and shorter holidays among its showroom staff. Demands for sacrifices by some of the company's lowest-paid workers contrast with a £205,000 increase, to £475,000, just awarded to Mr Brown. Pay rises for the executive directors were announced only days after the company unveiled an increase in charges to customers. The basic pay for showroom staff was £13,000, rising to £17,000 with long service and commission.

(The Times, 16 December 1994)

In Britain, throughout 1995, there was controversy over the enormous salaries paid to senior executives of large businesses. In addition to their absolute pay being high (in some cases over £1 million a year), they were seen to be taking high pay increases, of perhaps 50%, when ordinary workers in their businesses were being offered 2–5%. Why are some people paid so much more than ordinary workers? Economists would suggest that it is because there are very few people with the skills needed to head big companies. They have skills that are in great demand, but of which there is a very limited supply.

The shadow chancellor singled out Roger Urwin, chief executive of London Electricity plc, as getting a 14 per cent rise on his basic salary of £162,500 and other bonuses in his new contract . . . totalling £323,213.

(The Guardian, 6 April 1995)

The meaning of factors of production

In order for production to take place, four things are needed: **land**, **labour**, **capital** and **enterprise** (the latter sometimes also called **entrepreneurship**). These are called the **factors of production**.

Land

Any business needs somewhere to operate. This may be a large factory, a small office, a small stand selling newspapers, or just a desk. Any space that is used for carrying on a business activity will be seen by an economist as land.

Arid Bangladesh accuses India of choking Ganges

Bangladesh faces environmental and economic catastrophe across its entire southwestern region, a third of the country, because India has choked off most of the crucial dry-season flow of the once mighty Ganges. 'This is a life and death issue,' an internal government memorandum says. 'The survival of a nation is at stake.'

The livelihoods of 40 million people are in jeopardy. Parts of the country have turned to desert and climatic changes recorded. Parts of the Sunderbans, the world's largest mangrove forest, are dying. Thousands of fishermen are out of work and agriculture has been disrupted.

Ten thousand square miles of land have been salinated because the enfeebled Ganges cannot hold back seawater pushing upstream from the Bay of Bengal. Salt water now intrudes 136 miles inland . . .

The Ganges and rivers that flow off it are silting up, causing flooding in the rainy season. The Goria, once navigable even in the dry season, is dry for much of the year. 'We fear that because of the rise in the river bed the Ganges may change direction in the flood season,' a Bangladeshi government analyst said. 'This would be a catastrophe but it is only a matter of time.'

(The Times, 15 July 1994)

Labour

Any business needs workers of some kind. An accountant who is self-employed relies on their own mental effort to carry on their business, just as a labourer digging the road relies on their own physical effort. Any such mental or physical effort involved in carrying on a business will be seen by an economist as labour.

Capital

Any business needs money and equipment. A computer or a shovel, a pen or a drill, when used in carrying on a business, will be seen by an economist as capital. **Capital goods** (as opposed to **consumer goods**) are those goods that are used by a business to create other goods which will then be bought by consumers.

Enterprise

Any business needs someone with an *idea* about what that business will involve. It's no good having land, labour and capital without knowing what you want them for. The person who has the idea to start, say, a shop specialising in socks (i.e. Sock Shop) or a shop for ties (i.e. Tie Rack) is the entrepreneur, and that person brings a vital ingredient to the business: enterprise.

Some examples of the above factors of production would be:

- the computer being used to write this book: capital
- the person sitting writing this book: labour
- the publisher of this book: enterprise
- the room in which this book is being written: land
- a Conservative MP speaking in the House of Commons: labour

- the Ford motor factory at Dagenham: land
- a robot building a Ford Fiesta at Dagenham: capital

Rewards to the factors of production

Economists find it helpful to assume that businesses own nothing themselves but instead hire what they need from people who do own the factors of production. In return for the hire of these factors of production, the people who own them receive a relevant reward. This reward is based on how valuable and how difficult to come by are the particular factors.

Land and rent

Rent is paid to the owners of land. Land in some areas is very scarce, such as in the City of London, Central Manhattan or Hong Kong Island. In order to ration out who gets use of the land, rents are very expensive.

Labour and wages

Most people have the ability to do some form of work. Therefore labour is not particularly scarce, and so **wages** are not high. On the other hand, some people have skills that are quite rare, and these people will command high wages.

Note that *all* forms of payment for work will be known to an economist as wages, although they might be an accountant's fee, a teacher's salary or a car worker's wage.

The 'not too badly paid' explain why they are worth every penny

The Times **spoke to some of Britain's highest paid directors and asked them to explain the rationale behind their pay awards.**

Peter Wood, founder and chief executive of Direct Line, the insurance company, earned £18.2 million last year after the company's profits more than trebled to £50.2 million. Mr Wood has been so embarrassed by the publicity generated by his pay that he has negotiated a new contract. He will no longer receive multi-million-pound bonuses, but in compensation will receive a lump sum of £24 million.

Sir Christopher Bland, chairman of LWT, the broadcaster taken over by Granada last week, holds shares worth more than £14 million following the most lucrative 'golden handcuffs' deal in commercial broadcasting. Greg Dyke, his chief executive, has a stake worth £9.3 million. Sir Christopher defended the bonus scheme: 'It was not a windfall. It was a well-earned reward for all the genuine hard work involved in winning the franchise.'

(The Times, 4 March 1994)

Capital and interest

Businesses will need to borrow money to pay for equipment. The reward for *lending* such money is called **interest**. **Interest rates** (the cost of borrowing money) can go up or down. If the interest rate is high, it becomes less worthwhile to borrow money because any project will have to make more money than before to be profitable since more interest is now being paid.

Enterprise and profit

In return for having the idea that brings together the factors of production, the entrepreneur takes any money that the business has left after the other factors of production have received their rewards. This is called **profit**. In fact, to be exact, it is called **gross profit**. Taxes then have to be paid to the government, and the entrepreneur can then take anything that's left. This after-tax profit is called **net profit**.

Summary

The four factors of production are: land, labour, capital and enterprise. These factors of production are not owned by businesses but are hired by them. Rent is paid for land, wages for labour, interest for capital, and profit for enterprise. The level of reward depends upon the scarcity of the particular factor of production. A computer programmer has rare skills whereas most people would be able to pack shelves in a supermarket. So, they are paid differently depending on the scarcity of their skills or abilities. Labour is generally less well rewarded than the other factors of production because while land, capital and enterprise are relatively scarce, labour (or at least unskilled labour) is relatively plentiful.

chapter 8

MAKES YOU THINK!

1 Who would you expect to receive the highest wages out of the following:

   (a) a shelf-stacker at Tesco
   (b) a checkout operator in Marks & Spencer
   (c) a computer programmer for J Sainsbury?

2 Why are they paid differently?
3 The owners of which factors of production are paid more than others? Try to put them in order.

Chapter 9

Businesses: their costs, revenue and profit

Billionaire Warren Buffett, who has just written-down his investment in USAir, believes it is far from certain the deeply troubled US airline will succeed in reaching a much needed cost reducing agreement with its labour unions.

USAir . . . has been talking to its unions for months about how to slash its labour costs. Wall Street analysts believe an agreement is essential if USAir is to avoid . . . bankruptcy.

(Daily Telegraph, 21 March 1995)

The meaning of costs

As with many other words, economists use the term 'costs' in a very specific way. The cost of production, for any business, is what could have been done with the resources used if they had been used differently – i.e. the opportunity cost. This suggests that the word 'cost' has a different meaning in economics from that understood by accountants.

Economists look at the following opportunity costs involved in running a business:

Labour costs

A painter and decorator is likely to be self-employed. When working out their costs for the accountant, costs of materials, petrol for transport and insurance payments will be entered, and as long as the total income received is greater than the costs, the decorator will consider that a profit has been made. However, what has not been included is the value of the time that has been spent doing the job. This will have an opportunity cost, because something else could have been done during that time. Economists would therefore want to include the price of labour as a cost.

Capital costs

A small business may be started with £10,000 of the entrepreneur's own money. If that money were not invested in the business, it could be saved and could earn interest instead. The loss of the opportunity to earn that interest must therefore be regarded as a cost for the economist.

Depreciation

Any property owned by a company will lose value over a period of time. This is called **depreciation**. Equipment has a limited life span and so, after a period of time, will need replacing. Think about a car. Most cars have a life span of around 10 years, so a car costing £10,000 would therefore be worth almost nothing after 10 years. One way to think of this would be to knock £1,000 off its value each year, but this is unrealistic: approximately 40% of the value of a new car is lost after one year. Therefore, after owning the car for one year, the business could sell the car for £6,000. That is the opportunity cost of owning the car: if the car were not owned by the business, they could have had £6,000 instead. (There are, however, exceptions to this rule. Buildings that are kept in good repair can last a very long time, and indeed actually *increase* in value over a period of time – i.e. as with works of art, they **appreciate**.)

Goodwill, recognition and brand loyalty

A business will only stay in business if it has a good reputation. This will be built up over a period of time by giving customers what they want: either cheap or good-value products, a reliable service or high standards. When people are thinking of using a particular type of business, they will go to a name they know – particularly long-established brand names such as Phillips, Nestlé or Jaguar. Therefore, if a business is to be sold, it is not just the buildings and equipment that is paid for: it is the *image* of the business as well; and if this image is not sold also, the amount that someone is willing to pay for the goodwill, recognition or brand loyalty is being gone without – another opportunity cost.

Fixed and variable costs

A **fixed cost** is often referred to in business as an **overhead**. Fixed costs are costs that the business has to pay whether it produces anything or not. Think about somebody starting up as a hairdresser. Certain items will have to be purchased before any customers can be seen – for example, scissors, combs and brushes will be needed. If the hairdresser sees one customer, 10 customers or no customers during a week, the scissors, combs and brushes will still have to be paid for. If a shop is being used, rent for the shop will have to be paid, as will charges for heating and lighting. These will all be fixed costs.

In this example, other things such as hair shampoo or conditioners will also need to be bought, but the quantities of these that are bought will depend on the number of customers seen. The costs of these latter items are therefore called **variable costs**.

Consider an aeroplane flying from Frankfurt to New York. Whether it carries one passenger or 500, most of the costs involved in flying that aeroplane still have to be paid, namely landing fees, fuel bills, pay for the flight crew. These are the fixed costs. On the other hand, some costs will rise as more passengers are carried. These are the variable costs. In this example, food and drink may be the only variable costs. The price charged to a passenger could be very low (such as when flights are discounted), and it would still make sense to carry the passenger. As long as you can cover the variable costs and a little bit more, it makes sense to sell a place on the flight: even £1 in excess of the variable costs is £1 towards the fixed costs that have to be paid whether or not that passenger flies.

Similarly, cross-channel ferry companies may offer you the chance to have a day out in France for £1. This usually applies in winter when there is a lot of spare space. The ferry would normally run perhaps half-full, and again virtually all the costs are fixed – they will have to be paid whether you sail or not. So your £1 is revenue that goes to offset those fixed costs. However, the ferry company also hopes that you will spend extra money in the bars, the cafeterias and the duty-free shop so that they gain more revenue!

Total and average costs

When the fixed costs are added to the variable costs, we arrive at the **total cost**. The total cost is the sum of all the costs of the business. If we then divide the total cost by the **total output**, we find the **average cost**. So, if a plane is carrying just one passenger, then the average cost of the flight will be the same as the total cost. However, if the plane is carrying 500 passengers, the average cost will be the total cost of the flight divided by 500. The airline will want the fare charged to be greater than the average cost, but this will be impossible if only a few people are flying. As more people fly, however, the average cost will decrease until it is equal to the fare (at which point the company **breaks even**). Thereafter, as yet more tickets are sold, the money that is received from each fare will be *greater* than the average cost.

Marginal cost

In economics, marginal simply means *extra*. So the **marginal cost** for the airline is the extra cost of carrying one extra customer. We have already seen that this is very low compared with the average cost of a passenger because the marginal cost only takes into account the variable costs, while the average cost is calculated using the total cost.

A useful way to think about the relationship between average and marginal costs

Think about a football team whose average score in the season so far is 2 goals per match. Any score they get in their *next* game will be their marginal (i.e. extra) score. If this marginal score is less than 2, their average score will go down. If this marginal score is greater than 2, their average score will rise. If they score exactly 2, the marginal and average scores will be the same.

It is the same with costs. If the marginal cost is less than the average cost, then the average cost will fall. If the marginal cost is greater than the average cost, then the average cost will rise.

The **marginal cost curve** will always cross the **average cost curve** at the average cost curve's *lowest point* – see Figure 9.1.

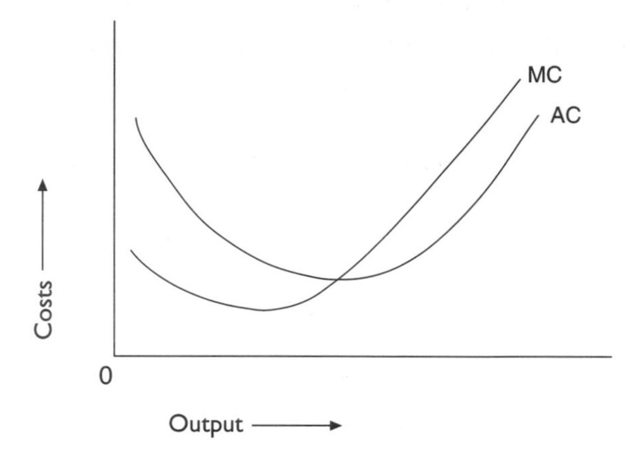

Figure 9.1 The average cost curve and the marginal cost curve

The troubled £10.5 billion Channel Tunnel warned earlier this week, that it was on the verge of collapsing from the weight of £2 million a month interest payments on its £8 billion debt.

(Adapted from The Guardian, 13 April 1995)

Compared to the Channel Tunnel, cross-channel ferry companies have a high proportion of variable costs. They have large crews and use a lot of fuel. Each crossing is expensive. The Channel Tunnel, on the other hand, is relatively cheap to operate. Most of the Tunnel's costs are fixed in that the cost of the original engineering product must be paid whether passengers use the Tunnel or not.

Total, average and marginal revenue

Money that the airline receives in fares will be its **revenue**. Revenue is thus the money that a business receives from the sale of its goods or services. As Mr Micawber may have said: if revenue exceeds costs, good; if costs exceed revenue, disaster. **Total revenue** is all the money received from sales. **Average revenue** is total revenue divided by the number of sales; so, if British Airways receives £150,000 from the sale of 500 tickets for a flight from London to New York, the average revenue from each ticket is £300. **Marginal revenue** is the money received from selling one extra unit of output; for British Airways, this will involve selling one extra seat.

When is it worthwhile remaining in operation?

We have an aircraft that is going to fly to New York, but only 200 people have booked seats. Most of the costs, however, are still going to have to be paid. We can't ask those passengers who have already booked their seats to pay more for their tickets. However, what we can do is sell tickets more cheaply to try to fill some extra seats. Cheaper tickets might not cover the average price of carrying a passenger, but that doesn't matter: as long as it doesn't cost us more to carry a passenger than we receive for their ticket, it makes sense to take them anyway, even at a ridiculously cheap fare. So, at least in the short run, it makes sense for a firm to carry on producing so long as its marginal revenue (in this example, the price of a cheaper ticket for one extra passenger) is greater than its marginal cost (in this example, the (variable) cost of carrying one extra passenger). This is because in the short run, some costs are fixed and some are variable. That in fact is the definition of 'the short run' in economics: that you have both fixed and variable costs. In the long run, you can get rid of your fixed costs, so that *all* your costs become variable. Businesses continue to operate in the short run even when they are making a loss, because they would have to pay their fixed costs even if they closed down. While they continue in operation, however, they can raise revenue that will cover their variable costs and at least make a contribution to fixed costs.

How long is the short run?

Think about a trader who sells hot dogs in the market. He has fixed costs: the repayments for the loan he took out to buy the stand; and he has variable costs: the costs of the sausages, rolls, onions and mustard. He can get rid of his fixed costs quite quickly by simply selling the stand and paying off his loan. Thus, the long run here is the time it takes to sell the stand – perhaps a day.

Compare that situation with a car manufacturer such as Vauxhall at Luton. If this manufacturer were to stop production, the company would have a huge factory to sell. It may be able to sell the land, but this could take months or years, and in the meantime, rent would still have to be paid until the site was sold, workers may need to be paid until their notice expired, and so forth. The short run for Vauxhall could therefore last months or years.

Simon shrinks losses to £18m

Simon Engineering, the access equipment to process engineering group, turned in reduced losses of £18m last year, down from £160m in 1993.

Over the past year, Simon has sold eight subsidiaries, closed four more, and sold a number of properties.

(Daily Telegraph, 21 March 1995)

Profit

Very simply, profit is a business's total revenue minus its total costs. That is very straightforward, but I'm afraid economists complicate things a bit. Remember that we said at the beginning of the chapter that economists were interested in opportunity costs. Similarly here, when it comes to profit, if a business made £10 million last year but could have made £6 million from doing something else, then that £6 million is the opportunity cost for the firm. The £6 million here would be called **normal profit**. Economists count normal profit as a cost.

If a business cannot make normal profit, then it switches to doing something else. Economists assume that any business will do the thing that it can make the most money by doing. Thus, normal profit is the amount of profit needed to *keep* a business doing what it is doing rather than switching to something else. Any profit that is made over and above normal profit is called **abnormal**, **supernormal** or **economic profit** – they all mean the same thing. In this example £6 million is normal profit and the remaining £4 million is supernormal or economic profit.

Because economists treat normal profit as a cost (it's something that a business has to cover), abnormal profit is something that is made whenever total revenue is *greater* than total cost.

Summary

Economists are interested in opportunity cost rather than financial cost. Businesses face both fixed and variable costs in the short run, but in the long run *all* costs are variable.

The total cost is equal to the fixed costs plus the variable costs, while the average cost is the total cost divided by the level of output. The marginal cost is the cost of producing one extra unit of whatever the business produces.

Revenue is the money received from sales, and profit is any revenue that is greater than total cost. Normal profit is the amount of profit that makes it worthwhile for a business to carry on doing what it is doing rather than switch to something else. Abnormal profit is profit that is greater than normal profit.

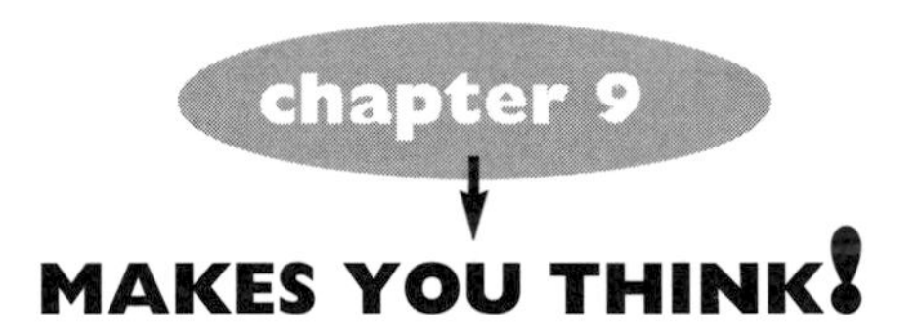

The troubled £10.5 billion Channel Tunnel warned earlier this week, that it was on the verge of collapsing from the weight of £2 million a month interest payments on its £8 billion debt.

(Adapted from The Guardian, 13 April 1995)

1. What are the fixed costs of operating the Channel Tunnel?
2. If you were advising Eurotunnel (the company that operates the Tunnel) on fares to charge, what would be your advice?
3. Sarah Mitchell owns a brasserie. Explain whether the following costs are likely to be fixed or variable:

   (a) rent
   (b) the wages of her chef
   (c) the wages of casual staff
   (d) ingredients for dishes
   (e) cooking pans
   (f) interest payments on her start-up loan

Chapter 10

Economies of scale

In 1994, the British Secretary of State for the Environment, John Gummer, announced a change of attitude towards out-of-town shopping centres. Throughout the 1980s and early 1990s, the 'superstore' became a feature of the outskirts of most medium-size and large towns. People appreciate the convenience of driving to one store where they can park their car, do all their shopping, load it into the car and drive home; and businesses in turn – as we shall see in this chapter – like to provide the facility of a big store. So why has the Secretary of State now turned against such developments in UK towns?

For centuries, the main town in each regional area of the UK was known as the 'market town'. People from outlying villages would meet in the market town centre to do their shopping. The marketplaces in towns like Norwich are natural central points. Similarly, today, you could walk down the 'high street' in any major town and expect to find all the shops you would want. The problem, however, for stores such as Sainsbury, Tesco, Dixons and Currys has been that there is no more room to expand. Therefore, such stores have been keen to build on cheap land outside the towns.

The issue for the community is that if people can do all or most of their shopping 'out of town' they will have no more reason to visit the town centre. As a result, shops in the town centre will have fewer customers and will close down, giving people even less reason to visit the centre of town. Over time, the town centres will thus become empty spaces. To put it more emotionally, towns are having their hearts ripped out. Of course, not everybody has the use of a car. So where do *they* go for their shopping? Which groups of people are particularly affected by this problem?

Cant and convenience

. . . The supermarkets that now open seven days a week have been picking up market share from the independents – the family-owned butchers and greengrocers.

Of course, this is not merely a function of Sunday trading. Economies of scale have allowed the big boys to undercut the small stores, and they have also extended their range to newspapers, pharmacy goods and cut flowers, thereby offering shoppers an entire high street under one roof.

But Sunday trading has undoubtedly played its part. Some convenience stores – the ones not driven out of business – now only open their doors after 4 pm on a Sunday, because it is simply not worth being open at the same time as the multiples.

Forget the cant about consumer choice. The real motivation behind 'freeing up' Sunday trading came from a big business community prepared to flout the law in order to get what it wanted. And it has worked.

(The Guardian, 20 May 1995)

Economies of scale are those advantages that businesses such as superstores can gain from greater size, and which may enable those businesses to charge lower prices than would otherwise be the case. However, is this always best for the consumer and for society?
In this issue, as with many in economics, there are both 'gainers' and 'losers' involved.

The meaning of economies of scale

'Economies of scale' is another of those phrases that sounds complicated and off-putting but isn't really. In everyday English, when somebody is making savings, they are **economising** or **making economies**. So, another word for economies is **savings**. 'Scale' is an alternative word for size. Therefore, 'economies of scale' simply means 'savings from size'. And that's it!

We saw in the last chapter that for any business, some costs are fixed while others vary with the level of output. Economies of scale serve to reduce a business's average cost (the total cost divided by the total output). This average cost will fall as output goes up since fixed costs now account for an ever-smaller proportion of the total cost.

Internal and external economies of scale

Internal economies of scale are those advantages that a business gains as it grows larger. **External economies of scale** refer to the advantages that a business receives not as a result of its own growth but owing to the fact that the whole industry is expanding. For example, one of the reasons that so many computer and information-technology businesses set up along the M4 Corridor (an area running along the M4 between London and Bristol) in England and in Silicon Valley in California was that other businesses in the same industry were *already* there. This meant that there was a pool of skilled labour available to be recruited (or poached) from other employers.

Types of internal economies of scale

Let's return to the superstores which we considered in the introduction for this chapter. If we compare a superstore with a small corner shop, we will see that the superstore has a number of ways to keep its average costs below those of the small corner shop.

The most obvious difference is that the superstore can buy in bulk. A small corner shop will buy the things it wishes to sell from the **wholesaler**. Large supermarket chains, on the other hand, do not need a wholesaler: they will arrange contracts directly with manufacturers. Fresh fruit and vegetables, for example, are supplied from the farm direct to regional distribution centres for immediate dispatch to stores. The buying power of Sainsbury and Tesco is such that farms must produce to their specifications. If the quality is not good enough, the superstore company will quickly switch to an alternative supplier. Not only do they have the power to dictate standards of quality, but they can also dictate price. If the farms don't like the price that Sainsbury or Tesco are prepared to pay, they could refuse to supply, but where else are they going to offload the huge quantities that they have been growing specifically for the superstores? These advantages to the large business are called **purchasing economies**.

Another difference is that for a small shop to advertise on television would be prohibitively expensive. However, large companies such as Sainsbury and Tesco in the UK or Horten and

Kaufhof in Germany own so many stores that for their businesses to advertise on television works out at an acceptable cost per store. Also, these stores can afford to employ marketing specialists who design adverts and dream up special promotions. In the small shop, on the other hand, any advertising is likely to be done by the manager or owner with a felt-tip pen.

Furthermore, as a vast range of goods are stocked in the large superstore, Tesco and Sainsbury can introduce schemes to encourage customers to do all their shopping with them, such as cards that offer a discount when you spend over a certain amount.

These advantages to the large business are called **marketing economies**.

Another big difference between superstores and small shops is the technology employed. In a small shop, a traditional till will be used to ring up the price of each item bought; and if somebody is only buying six items, this does not take too long. However, in Sainsbury and Tesco, it is often not six but 60 items that are being purchased in one go. It used to take a long time to ring up each price on the till, and large queues at the checkouts were a common feature of Saturday-morning shopping. While there are still queues at certain times in Sainsbury and Tesco, they are now much reduced, however, because of the use of optically read bar codes. Most products show a little box in which is written a product identification number. This number is written in a form (i.e. the bar code) that can be read by laser scanning. This laser scan at the checkout feeds straight into a computer that quickly identifies the correct price for that product. This technology speeds up 'customer throughput'; and more customers equals more money being spent.

Other technological advantages are also available to superstores, such as more efficient refrigeration.

These advantages to large businesses are called **technical economies**.

Yet another difference between superstores and small shops is in the use of staff. In a very small shop, the shopkeeper will be responsible for buying the stock, keeping the accounts, doing any advertising, and probably looking after the till. In a superstore, on the other hand, there will be a number of specialist managers who will be responsible for, and have expertise in, a particular area. A Sainsbury store, for example, may have a bakery manager and a fresh-produce manager, as well as checkout supervisors and personnel management, and at head office, there will be marketing, strategy and accounts departments etc. The ability to employ specialists who can concentrate on a small part of the business's activity is essential for an efficient operation.

These advantages to large businesses are called **managerial economies**.

A further big difference between small shops and superstores is that Tesco and Sainsbury find it much easier to raise finance than would the Joe Bloggs Corner Shop. A small shop is likely to have to borrow from a bank any money that it needs for the purchase of major pieces of new equipment, and from a bank's point of view, a small shop is not the safest of businesses to which to lend money. To reflect this, the interest rate for repayments of any loans is likely to be high.

On the other hand, Sainsbury or Tesco make so much profit in any one year that they are unlikely to need to borrow money for new projects. However, if they do need to do so, they are so unlikely to go out of business that banks will be keen to lend them money, and so a low rate of interest will be charged.

These advantages to large businesses are called **financial economies**.

Have you noticed how superstores have

started selling a wider range of goods than just food recently? Clothes, stationery, newspapers, magazines, perfume and lottery tickets are all now available at my local Sainsbury superstore. Small shops, on the other hand, are unable to carry anything like the range of products that are available at the superstore. The sale of food is a fairly stable market: people always buy food as a priority. But other markets can fall off over time. The market for tobacco products, for example, has declined steeply over the last 30 years. Large businesses try to insure against their products becoming unwanted by selling a wide range of things so that if demand for one thing goes down, the business still makes money by selling other things instead. The tobacco industry is a classic example. Faced with falling sales of cigarettes, the industry has responded on the one hand by developing new markets – selling its lethal tubes to people in developing countries, where, as the life expectancy is low anyway, the effects of smoking are less obvious – and on the other hand 'diversifying' by selling completely different products also. One example of this was British American Tobacco, changing its name to BAT Industries and buying the Eagle Star insurance company.

These advantages to large businesses are called **risk bearing economies**.

Diseconomies of scale

We have now seen that large businesses enjoy lower average costs than do small businesses – at least, this is generally the case. However, certain disadvantages can arise if a business becomes too large. For a start, communications can become a problem. 'Little empires' develop in large businesses where groups are more interested in what benefits them than in what benefits the business as a whole. Furthermore, workers in a large business can feel alienated (distant) from the owners of the business. Workers in a small shop are likely to feel more loyalty to their owner than does a Sainsbury checkout assistant to the Sainsbury brothers.

Disadvantages to businesses from growing too big are called **diseconomies of scale**, and they result in a U-shaped average cost curve that looks as shown in Figure 10.1.

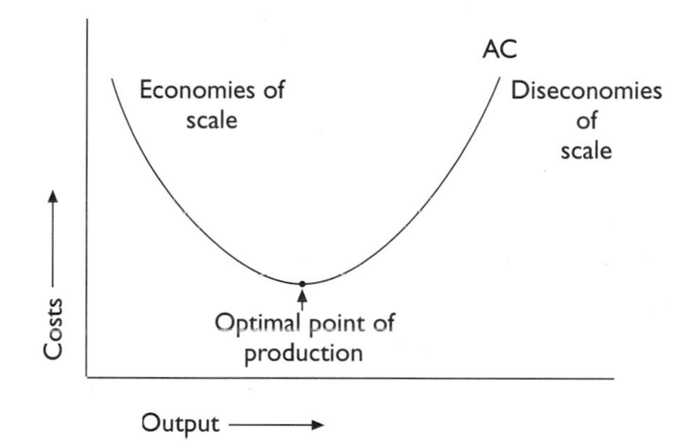

Figure 10.1 The U-shaped average cost curve caused by diseconomies of scale

Note that the best place to produce, i.e. the point of *lowest* average cost, is at the bottom of the curve, and this point is called the **optimum point of production**. Some companies have actually tried to get to the optimum point of production by becoming smaller – one example in the early 1990s was ICI which split itself into two separate companies. However, it is still more common for companies to merge in order to take advantage, instead, of economies of scale. In 1995, for example, the two drug companies Glaxo and Welcome merged because they produced the same sorts of product. Now they only need one set of managers and one set of research and development staff.

Why do small businesses still survive?

Most people in the UK are employed in small businesses, defined as those employing less than 50 people. Indeed, many people work for businesses that employ only one or two people. Certain businesses would find little advantage in growth. This is usually the case if fixed costs are very low. For example, a hairdresser who visits clients in their home may not find a great advantage in being part of a larger organisation.

Summary

Economies of scale can be internal or external. Internal economies of scale can be: technical, managerial, purchasing, marketing, financial or risk bearing. If a business becomes too large, however, diseconomies of scale can set in.

The optimum point of production lies at the lowest point of the average cost curve.

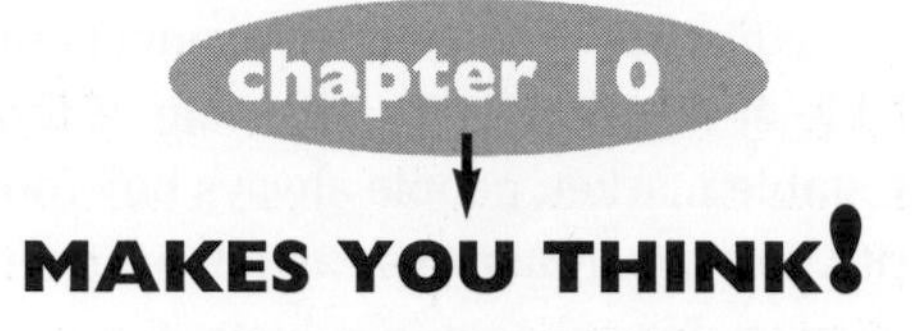

1. In two columns headed 'Gainers' and 'Losers', note down as many groups/types of people as you can think of who are affected by a smaller number of independent shops and a greater concentration of shopping in multiples.
2. Give an example of each of the internal economies of scale, from industries other than retailing.
3. Make a list of the types of business that tend to be small. What characteristics do you think they have in common, if any?

Chapter 11

Business ownership

Many of today's well-known businesses were started by one or two people, and the ownership of those businesses was very simple. However, during the nineteenth century, businesses wanted to expand and increase the number of owners. To do this they needed to sell **shares** (i.e. a share in the ownership of the business). To encourage people to buy shares, governments around the world passed laws which gave people **limited liability**. This will be explained later. During the twentieth century, many people bought shares in successful businesses for two reasons. One reason was to have a share in the profit made by the business. The second reason was the hope that a profitable business would attract more and more people to buying shares and that this increase in demand would push up the price, so that the shares could then be sold at a profit.

J Sainsbury was originally an independent grocer's shop owned by Mr J Sainsbury. Over a long period of time, more Sainsbury shops were opened around the country, and as the business expanded, shares were given to the family. Only the Sainsbury family owned these shares, and the shares could only be sold to other members of the family. At this stage, Sainsbury was a **private limited company**. During the 1980s, however, Sainsbury found that it needed to raise more money to pay for new superstores. To raise this money, it decided to sell shares to members of the public by **floating** the company on the **stock exchange**. The company now became a **public limited company**: J Sainsbury plc.

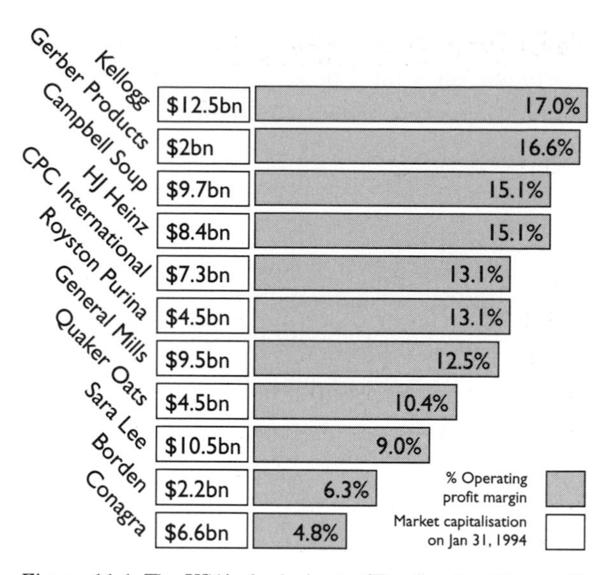

Figure 11.1 The USA's food giants (The Sunday Times, 21 August 1994)

Notice how many of the biggest food businesses shown in Figure 11.1 are named after a founder. These are all now owned by **shareholders**, however.

Sole traders

The simplest form of business ownership is the **sole trader**. Here, one person owns the business, takes all the decisions and risks their own money. Many people enjoy being self-employed and are happy to have complete control of their own business. However, there is nobody to share the responsibilities involved in decision-making, and raising finance is a problem.

Sole traders usually finance their business through a **bank loan**. However, banks will only lend if they believe that the business is likely to be successful. Furthermore, because they are not sure that the business will be able to keep up loan repayments, the banks will charge a high rate of interest. And as a final safeguard, a bank will ensure that it can get its money back, if the loan is not repaid, by requiring **security** on the loan. This normally means that if you have a mortgage on your home for £20,000 and your home is valued at £70,000, then the bank will consider that there is £50,000 value left in your home. They will therefore loan you up to £50,000 providing that you agree that the bank can have your house if you cannot repay the £50,000.

Sole traders are personally liable for any debts they have, even if they are not the trader's fault. For example, a trader may do a job for a larger business. The job may be worth £10,000, but this will not be paid until the job is complete. In order to complete the job, the sole trader must spend £8,000 on equipment and materials. Unfortunately, when the job is complete, the larger business closes down and the £10,000 is never paid. However, the sole trader still has to cover the £8,000 already spent because the sole trader has **unlimited liability**. This situation happens all too often!

Partnerships

Sometimes, a pair or a small group of people will get together to run a business. This is called a **partnership**. Examples are often to be found amongst lawyers and accountants, because people with different areas of expertise in these areas can join together to share a building and share support staff. For example, in a law firm, one solicitor may specialise in criminal law, another in family law, and another in company law.

Partnerships face unlimited liability in the same way as do sole traders. However, it is slightly easier to raise money here as each partner in turn will be required to pay a sum of money to 'buy into' the partnership. On the other hand, each partner is also responsible for any debts run up by any of the other partners. So, if one partner orders a yacht for £1 million and uses it to sail into the sunset, the other partners are liable for the payment of the £1 million.

There is one small exception to the unlimited-liability rule in a partnership. Somebody may be a **silent partner**. That is to say that they put some money into the partnership in return for a share of the profits but take no part in the running of the partnership, do not work for it and have absolutely no say in any decisions. Under these circumstances, it is only the money that has been invested that is liable to be used to pay off any debts. A silent partner therefore only has limited liability.

Private and public limited companies

The technical name for both a private and a public limited company is a **joint stock company**. This simply means that the stock in a company is owned jointly by several people. Notice, too, that for the first time we have introduced the term **company** when talking about a business. This is because a 'company' is a very special form of business. A sole trader or a partnership has no special place in law. If I start up a business, I own all the property and all the debts. I can describe the car that I buy to carry out my business as a company car, but as far as the law is concerned it is my car. On the other hand, a company has a separate legal existence from the people who own it. If a company buys a car, it is the company that owns it, not any of the shareholders.

A company is owned by the shareholders, who elect a board of directors to run the company on their behalf. In a private limited company (which can have 2–50 shareholders), the directors will often be the same people as the shareholders. The liability of the shareholders here is limited to the money that they have used to buy shares. In other words, if I buy £2,000 worth of shares in a company and that company then goes out of business leaving many unpaid bills, I will not get my £2,000 back but nor can I be asked to pay any of the bills: The *company* owes that money, not me.

A public limited company is similar to a private one except that its shares are traded on the stock exchange. Members of the public can buy these shares by going through a **stockbroker** or bank. Technically, owning shares gives you the right to attend the annual shareholders' meeting and vote, but in reality large financial institutions own large percentages of shares in any public company, and so it is they who have the voting power.

As a shareholder, you will generally receive a share of the profit each year (i.e. a **dividend**), and you can watch the price of your shares going up or down according to changes in demand for that company's shares – share prices are given in newspapers each day. Again, you of course have limited liability here.

Five directors of Maid, the on-line information supplier whose shares tumbled soon after its flotation a year ago, yesterday sold a 4.3% stake in the company for £2.64m. The sale cuts Maid directors' holding to 42%.

(Daily Telegraph, 21 March 1995)

Before the **flotation** of Maid on the stock exchange, the directors owned all the shares. Now they only own 42%. Maid has thus switched from being a 'Ltd' to being a 'Plc'.

The private and public sectors

So far, we have looked at the main types of business ownership in the **private sector**, i.e. at businesses owned by individuals in some way. However, the *government* is also the owner of certain businesses. In the UK, it is becoming increasingly difficult to find examples of such businesses in the **public sector**, but the Post Office is one, and so it is known as a **public corporation**. Local authorities also run some businesses, such as some local leisure centres.

Summary

Private-sector businesses can be: sole traders, partnerships, private limited companies or public limited companies. A company is owned by shareholders but has a separate legal existence from the people who own it.

Limited liability applies to shareholders in companies and to silent partners. It places a limit on the amount of money that these people stand to lose if the business fails.

Some business activity is carried on by the government, and this forms the public sector.

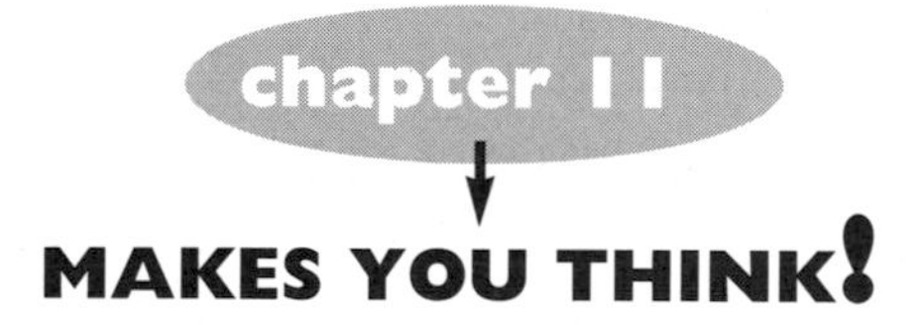

Explain:

1. Why is trust very important in a partnership?
2. With limited liability, who are the losers?
3. How might the goals of managers be different from those of shareholders?

Chapter 12

The aims of business

In his *Troubleshooter* books, Sir John Harvey-Jones, the former chief executive of ICI, gives several examples of where he has given advice to businesses that would make them more profitable. This advice has often been rejected because it would involve the business organisation in doing things that it does not wish to do. Examples of businesses reluctant to wholeheartedly adopt his advice range from a small apple-juice business in England to a bus manufacturer in Hungary. Now you may be saying that what a business wants to do is to make money, and that any business that rejected Sir John's advice must therefore think that it knows better how to make money. That may be true, but it is also apparent that making money, while certainly an important aim of business, is not the only aim.

Profit maximisation

Remember that in economics, we sometimes have to make assumptions. We may know that making as much profit as possible is not the only aim of business, but it nonetheless helps us to predict how a business may behave if we *do* assume that all businesses try to maximise their profits. In Chapter 10 we found that the optimal point of production was at the bottom of the average cost curve where average costs are at their lowest, and we might now assume that businesses will want to produce at this point to keep their costs low.

However, this might not always be the case. For example, the management of the business may like controlling a large empire, and for this reason may have no desire to reduce output in order to cut out diseconomies of scale.

The separation of ownership and control

Public companies are owned by shareholders who have no part in the running of the company. Although the shareholders elect the board of directors, this is usually a process of existing directors nominating either each other or their friends. Remember that the vast majority of shares are owned by financial institutions such as banks, insurance companies and pension funds. These institutions are often successful in getting their own directors elected as directors of companies that have no prior connection with the finance industry.

Directors hire managers to run the business from day to day. Managers (and executive directors) make the decisions and control the company. The owners of the company (the shareholders) do not have enough information to know whether the profits of the company are being maximised. Managers and directors have every incentive to run the company in their own interests rather than with the aim of making as much profit as possible for the shareholders. Indeed, managers and directors may seek to maximise their salaries, their free time, their expenses, their company cars, their team of secretaries, and so on. However, the management of a company cannot ignore their shareholders. They must make enough profit to keep their shareholders satisfied with them, or the shareholders might elect new directors or sell to another company promising more profit. Paying to shareholders the amount needed to keep them satisfied is called **profit satisficing** and is an alternative to profit maximising.

In the spring of 1995, Trafalgar House made a takeover bid for Northern Electric, the supplier of electricity to homes in the north of England. They offered shareholders a sum of money for each share that was much more than the price being offered for the shares in normal trading on the stock exchange. In response to this, the directors of Northern Electric offered all their shareholders a cash payout, thus proving that these directors had not been maximising the dividend to shareholders.

Summary

Profit maximisation may not be the only aim of a business. In public companies, there is a separation of ownership and control, so that directors and managers may run a company in their own interests. However, the directors and managers must nonetheless keep their shareholders satisfied with their performance.

chapter 12

MAKES YOU THINK!

1. A survey by American Express revealed that British executives have spent so much time trying to outwit restrictions placed on their travel allowances that the cost of the time involved was greater than any financial savings made. Do you think there would be much difference in the attitude to expenses of a businesswoman who owned her own business and of a manager within that business?
2. British industry is often criticised for **short-termism**: looking for short-term profits rather than being willing to wait for greater returns over many years. How might this criticism be applied to the ownership of large PLCs?
3. Stakeholders are the different groups of people affected by the activities of a business. Who might be the stakeholders in British Telecom (BT)?

Chapter 13

The benefits of competition

Research produced in April 1995 by Kleinwort Benson Securities reveals that UK hotels saw a big increase in their profits in 1994. This was accompanied by a decrease in hotel rooms of 1,412 – or the equivalent of 32 hotels. This may appear strange because, as this chapter will suggest, where an industry is making profits, new businesses will set up in that market, and higher profits should equal *more* new hotels rather than fewer. What actually happened was that 134 hotels closed down while 102 new hotels opened that were better suited to what 1990s travellers are seeking. It is the old, small hotels in towns that are closing, while roadside lodges such as Forte's 'Travel Lodge' are proving the popular alternative: according to *The Guardian*, 'They have established brand credibility. People know what they will be getting and how much they will have to pay.' On the other hand, small businesses will not completely disappear from the industry: '. . . there are still a lot of people who sell their houses when they retire and set up small businesses' (both quotes taken from *The Guardian*, 6 April 1995).

The meaning of perfect competition

Economists describe a theoretical type of market which is known as **perfect competition** and is the opposite of a monopoly (see Chapter 18). While it may be unrealistic to look for examples of markets which exactly fit the model of perfect competition, what should be said is that the nearer a market is to this model, the better the deal for the consumer. On the other hand, any *business* would prefer it if its competitors in the market were to disappear!

The characteristics of a perfectly competitive market are as follows:

- There must be many buyers and many sellers in the market, and none of them should be big/important enough to influence the price. The technical term is that they must all be **price takers** as opposed to a monopoly situation where a business can *set* the price. See Chapter 18)
- There are no barriers to entry or exit (see Chapter 14). This means that you will see new businesses setting up and others closing down quite routinely
- Both consumers and producers possess **perfect knowledge** of prices and other aspects such as quality and design. Although in reality it would never be the case that everyone has perfect knowledge, if consumers at least know that they can get something of the same quality and design more cheaply in another shop, they will go there instead. Consumers *without* that knowledge may indeed get 'ripped off'
- All businesses produce a **homogenous** product. This simply means that the products made by different producers cannot be distinguished. Here, **branding** becomes very important, because often one product can be identical to another except for the name on the packaging. Consumers will often be prepared to pay more for a brand associated with good quality

The perfectly elastic demand curve

As already mentioned, under perfect competition, businesses are price takers. If a business in a perfectly competitive market were to charge a price that is different from its competitors, one of two things would happen. If the price were lowered, revenue would straight away fall below costs (see Chapter 8) because of the highly competitive price (i.e. one just high enough to cover costs) that prevails. This is because if the price being charged was any higher than that which was just needed to cover costs, (normal profit is a cost); other firms would be able to undercut the price. On the other hand, if a business tried to raise prices, other firms would undercut that price, and all customers would then switch to those other firms. That is why any change in the prevailing price will result in no sales at all; and that gives us a perfectly elastic demand curve – see Figure 7.2.

Businesses and perfect competition

Businesses try to make life difficult for their competitors by:

- improving their product – and perhaps coming up with new products
- advertising
- creating a brand image

A restaurant owner is in a highly competitive market. The Warehouse Brasserie in Colchester is one of many restaurants in the town. It has marked itself out as being, in many people's opinion, the best restaurant in town by:

- serving food of consistently good quality
- serving food that is always interesting and tasty
- serving food at a relatively low price (when we go somewhere else for a change, we end up paying twice as much for an inferior meal)
- charging for the food rather than for fancy tablecloths and furniture (you eat on plain tables, and the seats are rather basic)

However, the main factor in the success of any restaurant is its *reputation*, and as it has been extremely difficult to get a table at the Warehouse for years, I guess it will now be almost impossible thanks to the enormous impact of this book!

Contestable markets

Contestable markets exist where there are no barriers to either entry to or exit from the market (see Chapter 14). Perfect competition can only apply where there are a large number of buyers and sellers in the market. However, the theory of contestable markets argues that even a small number of businesses in the market would be forced to act as if they were in perfect competition as long as it is easy for new businesses to enter the market and set up in competition. This is because, just as in perfect competition, any market where a business is making more than normal profit (i.e. the amount of profit necessary to make it worthwhile to stay in that market rather than do something else instead) will attract new competitors who will undercut existing prices. Therefore, existing businesses in a market will attempt to make it *difficult* for new businesses to enter the market. (This situation is detailed in the next chapter.)

Summary

Perfect competition is a theoretical position. Although it is difficult to think of any real-life markets that exactly match the theory, some will be much closer than others.

It is generally true that, the closer a market gets to the principles of perfect competition, the better for the consumer, whereas businesses find life to be easier when there is less competition because they can then raise their prices more easily.

The presence of competition ensures that in order to succeed, a business will have to keep its prices low and its product quality high. It also gives businesses an incentive to innovate – i.e. to come up with new ideas that their competitors do not have.

The theory of contestable markets implies that it is not the number of businesses that is important for consumer well-being so much as the ease with which new businesses may enter an existing market.

chapter 13

MAKES YOU THINK!

1. How competitive is the UK hotel industry (see the introduction to this chapter)?
2. Think of some industries that are in your view highly competitive. How does this affect their behaviour?
3. The Holiday Inn in Aachen, Germany, is one of several hotels in town trying to attract business customers. They have tried to encourage customers to book with them by lowering their price, but other hotels just lower their own prices in response. The hotel now markets itself as 'the friendliest hotel in Aachen', and so differentiates itself from the other hotels offering a similar product. How else might hotels try to make themselves different from the competition?

Chapter 14

Setting up and closing down

Daewoo is a Korean car company that, in 1995, tried to enter the UK car market for the first time. This is a difficult market to break into because there are already so many makes and models of car. Why should anybody want to buy a Daewoo instead?

Daewoo decided that it had to offer a product that was different from what was already available. There were not many ways in which they could make the design or equipment of the car special. Ford's **unique selling point** is the car phone included on all models, Volkswagen's is strength, Rover's is quality and BMW's is image. Daewoo decided to 'differentiate its product' by *service*. After conducting pre-launch market research and analysing the subsequent 200,000 responses, Daewoo found: that people wanted a combination of the safety features of the other producers in their new car; that people didn't like traditional car showrooms with 'pushy sales staff'; and that people didn't like the additional costs over and above the list price. Daewoo decided to try to break into the UK car market by making its unique selling point 'A car company that puts the customer first'. The company's tactic is to set up its own network of car centres where the manufacturer will sell direct to the customer and the sales staff will not be on commission.

Daewoo hopes that its 'manifesto' will help it to break into the UK car industry. How successful do you think the company will be?

Daewoo manifesto

1 **We deal direct.**
More for your money as standard on every Daewoo model:
- **Electronic ABS**
- **Driver's airbag**
- **Side impact protection**
- **Power steering**
- **Engine immobiliser**
- **Security glass etching**
- **Mobile phone**

2 **Hassle free buying.**
- **No salesmen on commission**
- **Fixed pricing**
- **No hidden charges**
- **Delivery included**
- **Number plates included**
- **Full tank of fuel**
- **12 months' road tax included**
- **Metallic paint included**

3 **Complete peace of mind.**
- **3 year/60,000 mile comprehensive warranty**
- **3 year/60,000 mile free servicing including parts and labour**
- **3 year free Daewoo Total AA Cover**
- **6 year anti-corrosion warranty**
- **30 day/1,000 mile money back or exchange guarantee**

4 **Courtesy servicing.**
- **Direct contact with mechanic who services your car**
- **Free courtesy car offered**
- **Pick up and return of your car offered**

(From a Daewoo advert in The Guardian, 1 April 1995)

The meaning of barriers to entry

Some industries are much easier for a business to set up in than are others. Things that make it difficult for new businesses to set up are called **barriers to entry**. These barriers are of the following types:

Legal barriers

There are laws that give existing businesses certain advantages. For example, in the UK you cannot decide to set up a television station and start to broadcast. Rather, **franchises** for different regions of the country are awarded by the Independent Television Commission (ITC). The same is true of radio, although pirate radio stations do exist and these are hunted down by the Department of Trade and Industry and the police. The limiting of television broadcasting is becoming very difficult to enforce, however, because the government cannot control satellites, only the ground headquarters.

Patents are used to prevent businesses from producing products that have been developed by another company. Patent rules (or intellectual property rights) are strictly enforced both by European Union countries and in North America. However, in the Far East there has been a tradition of reproducing Western products without the expense associated with research and development. Pirated CDs and videos are a clear breach of copyright law, as the money that is paid for them does not return to the original production company or featured artist. This unfair practice thus reduces the money available for future productions.

Capital costs

The amount of capital needed to set up a hairdressing business is quite small. If you are prepared to visit people in their own home, you may need a comb, scissors and brushes. Perhaps you will also need a range of shampoos and access to a car, but you could always use the customer's shampoo and get a taxi instead. Therefore, it is relatively easy, in terms of the capital needed, to start up as a hairdresser, which helps to explain why there are so many of them. On the other hand, the amount of capital needed to set up as a car producer in mass production is very high, and that helps to explain why there are just a few companies like Ford, Vauxhall (General Motors), the Rover Group, Peugeot and Nissan that produce cars in the UK.

Sunk costs

The Channel Tunnel provides a good example of **sunk costs**. These are costs which are not recoverable. The machinery that was used to build the Channel Tunnel can be sold second-hand, and so some of the production costs can be recovered. However, all of the labour costs, once paid, cannot be recovered. Once the tunnel was built, most of the costs of setting up the operation had already been paid. The sunk costs involved in setting up the Channel Tunnel were so high, however, that no one business would take it on, and a consortium of major companies eventually formed Eurotunnel.

A high level of sunk costs is an important barrier to entry, whereas a low level of sunk costs will encourage new businesses to have a go.

Economies of scale

In some industries, great advantages can be gained from being large (see Chapter 10). As it would take a long time for any new business to build up the size needed to gain these advantages, existing businesses will themselves be at a great advantage. British Telecom inherited a telephone network that had been developed over many decades. The cost of an extra line is very small. This is because the company operates on such a huge scale that its average costs are very low. On the other hand, a new business setting up in the telephone industry would face high average costs because the whole cost of its network would be divided between relatively few customers.

Marketing barriers

Just *knowing* of a business can often give it an advantage over an unknown competitor; and the longer a business has been operating, the more chance it has of being known. High spending on advertising and other forms of marketing helps to create customer awareness of a company or its products. Indeed, certain phrases have become synonymous with certain businesses thanks to expensive advertising. For example:

- 'The world's favourite airline' – British Airways
- 'Everything we do is driven by you' – Ford
- 'Vorsprung durch Technik' – Audi
- 'If only everything was as reliable as a' – Volkswagen

It takes a lot of time, effort and money to build up a 'brand image', which is a problem for new businesses trying to compete against existing brands. Virgin Cola is an example of a new product that did manage to break into a market with strong barriers to entry. However, it must be remembered that although this was a new brand of cola, the 'Virgin' brand name had already established an image both through the airline and, amongst the target market for cola, through record shops. The business also had large financial reserves to help it to market its cola against Coca-Cola and Pepsi.

In the UK, when Sainsbury introduced its 'Cola', the company was sued by Coca-Cola for the design of their cola cans. It was claimed by Coca-Cola that the Sainsbury can (which was sold at a much lower price than Coca-Cola's) was so close in design to a Coca-Cola can that it would mislead the public. As a result, Sainsbury was forced to change its design. Again here, it was the financial resources of the Sainsbury supermarket company that allowed it to market the product against Coca-Cola and Pepsi: a small business would not have been able to get over the barriers to entry.

Restrictive practices

Have you noticed that many small shops have an ice-cream cabinet that only stocks the Mars range of ice-cream bars? This is because Mars provides the freezer free of charge on the condition that it only be used to sell their products. This is one example of how established businesses can make it difficult for new entrants. Another is that businesses with a lot of money available in reserve may be willing to cut prices so that they make a loss for long enough to drive a new competitor out of business.

The professions have a successful way of keeping their prices high. For example, the number of solicitors is kept relatively small by the fact that to become a solicitor you have to register with the Law Society. This society is itself run by solicitors who ensure that only limited numbers qualify so that the supply of solicitors never outstrips demand and causes prices to fall.

The meaning of barriers to exit

Just as there can be problems for new businesses trying to enter an industry, so there can be problems for an established business trying to *leave* an industry. As we have found, to close down will often mean that no revenue can be raised to go towards 'sunk costs', whereas so long as the revenue that is raised is greater than any *additional* costs being incurred through operating, the business must carry on because any such additional revenue *can* be used to pay off these 'sunk costs'. This gives the Channel Tunnel a great advantage over ferry operators. It is true that the ferries themselves represent a large fixed cost for the ferry companies P&O and Sealink, but there are still high *variable* costs also involved every time a ferry puts to sea, such as fuel and staffing costs. On the other hand, Eurotunnel's main costs were built up while the tunnel was still being built, and the price of a new car ferry is quite insignificant in comparison. Eurotunnel can therefore afford to charge much lower prices than the ferries and still start to pay off some of the sunk costs. What stops it from doing this in its early years of operation is simply that there would not be enough capacity in the Tunnel to take everyone who would want to use the Tunnel if, as a result of Eurotunnel lowering its fares, the ferry companies were driven out of business.

Market concentration

The number of firms present in an industry will vary depending on the profitability of the industry and the nature of any barriers to entry and exit in that industry. Generally, industries fall into the following categories:

- **monopoly**: where there is only *one* supplier in a market – e.g. the Post Office
- **oligopoly**: where a small number of firms supply the market – e.g. petrol companies and banks
- **competitive**: where there are a large number of suppliers, none of which is large enough to dominate the market – e.g. . . . well, can you think of an example?

Summary

Barriers to entry will vary from one industry to another. These are the difficulties that exist for new businesses trying to start up in an industry.

Barriers to exit mean that it is sometimes difficult for a business to stop producing and leave an industry.

1 Compare the barriers to entry in the fast-food industry with the motor-car manufacturing industry.
2 How has the proliferation of satellite television channels affected barriers to entry in the broadcasting industry?
3 List some industries in which there may be important barriers to exit, and suggest what those barriers might be.

Part II
When the market fails

Public and merit goods

In the seventeenth century, the philosopher Thomas Hobbes wrote that without a strong central government, life would be 'nasty, brutish and short'. In those days, although people expected very little from their government, something they *did* expect was what only a strong government could give: security. Nowadays, we expect a lot more from government, but the 1980s in fact saw a move in many Western countries for governments to provide *less*. Indeed, Russia, together with Central and Eastern Europe, has seen massive 'privatisation' during the subsequent 1990s.

Portugal privatises

Portugal has sold 19.5 per cent of Banco Fomento e Exterior, the state owned trade bank, through the Lisbon stock exchange for 19.4 billion escudos (£77.3 million). The exchange said bidding for the shares was oversubscribed.

The shares will be quoted in Lisbon from January 2. Portugal aims to continue its privatisation programme by selling off stakes in Portugal Telecom and the production arm of EDP, the state electricity company.

(The Times, 28 December 1994)

Public goods

Even in a market economy, there is a need for the government to produce certain goods and services which there is no incentive for a private firm to produce. These are called **public goods**. One of the very basic roles of government is to provide public goods of defence together with law and order. Think about the armed forces. If a private firm provided a navy and offered to use it to protect anyone who paid for the service, how would it work? Would you be any less protected by it if you didn't pay? The same is true of the police. It would be impractical for the police to deter burglaries only from houses that have bought the service, or only to investigate the murders of those people who have paid for the murder-investigation service. The point here is that there are some things which it would be impractical for private firms to provide. Think also about street lights. Once they are provided, you cannot stop people who want to walk down the street from benefiting from those lights whether or not they have paid for them. Similarly, the fact that one person is benefiting from the light in no way diminishes the benefit available to someone else walking down the street.

Public goods, such as street lights, the armed forces and the police, therefore have two key characteristics. They are:

- non-excludable
- indivisible

Non-excludability simply means that once the good or (more likely) service is provided, it is not possible to stop people from benefiting from it. Indivisibility, or 'non-rivalry', means that the fact that one person is benefiting from what is being provided does not reduce the benefit available to somebody else.

Public goods are not free, and the government has the power to ensure that people *pay* for these goods through **taxes**. However, there are also many things provided by the government that are not public goods even though they are free at the point of delivery and are paid for out of taxes. Schools, for example, are not public goods, because clearly you can exclude non-payers from a school – as is the case with independent schools. Furthermore, it is often argued that an extra person in a class does reduce the attention available to everyone else. Similarly, health is not a public good since people again can be excluded who cannot pay (as in private hospitals), and one person having an operation clearly prevents other people using the operating theatre at the same time. Therefore, both education and health fail the non-excludability and the indivisibility (or non-rivalry) tests.

Merit goods

In the UK and many European countries, both education and health care are provided by the government for most people and paid for out of taxes. This is because governments have believed that people ought to have access to them. However, to what extent should people have their needs provided for by the government? We have noted that the USA does not have a National Health Service, but in the UK should dental treatment be freely available to everyone?

Things that are paid for either wholly or partly by the government, but which do not meet the criteria to be **public goods**, are called **merit goods**, and politicians disagree over what should be included as a merit good – e.g. should dental treatment be a merit good? Merit goods need not necessarily be provided free at the time of use. The government could decide to encourage people to use something by making it cheaper than it otherwise would be. For example, the UK government chooses to do this with some rail lines, giving the operator a **subsidy** to keep down fares and encourage people to use the service.

There are some things, on the other hand, which the government wishes to discourage people from buying, either by banning them (e.g. heroin) or by making them more expensive than they would otherwise be by adding a tax (e.g. on cigarettes). Goods which affect people harmfully when used are called **demerit goods**.

There follow some examples of things that, in Europe, are often paid for from taxes. Some are public goods and some are merit goods.

1 The Police
2 The Navy
3 The National Health Service
4 The Fire Brigade
5 The University of Brighton

1, 2 and 4 are public goods. These would never be provided by a private firm because it is impractical to exclude anybody from their benefit, and the fact that any one person has benefited from them does not diminish the benefit available to anyone else.

On the other hand, it *is* obviously possible to exclude people from hospital treatment or from a university, and the fact that a given person is benefiting from these resources does reduce the benefit available to other people. Therefore, whilst in many countries a health service and a higher-education system are provided by the government, both also can be, and are, provided by private businesses. These are therefore merit goods.

How are public and merit goods paid for?

As already mentioned, such services as health care and education have to be paid for by the government, which gets its money mainly from taxes. As the famous Chicago economist Milton Freeman said: 'There's no such thing as a free lunch.' Taxes can be divided into two types: **direct** and **indirect**. Direct taxes are charged directly on a person's income or wealth. The main ones here are income tax and national insurance. These taxes only apply to people earning above certain amounts. You may well not pay direct taxes, but you will almost certainly pay indirect taxes. These are taxes on what you spend, and the main one here is **value-added tax** (VAT). This tax is charged in all European Union countries, but the rate, and what it is charged on, differs. For example: in 1995, VAT in the UK was charged at 17.5% on everything you buy except food, children's-size clothes, books, newspapers and public transport. (Gas and electricity were taxed at 8%.) If you drive a car or motorbike, smoke tobacco or drink alcohol, you will be paying large additional taxes on these items, with leaded petrol being taxed more highly than unleaded.

Economists also describe taxes as **proportional**, **progressive** or **regressive**. A tax is proportional when the same percentage of tax is taken no matter how wealthy someone may be. A progressive tax is one where richer people pay a higher rate of tax than do poorer people. A regressive tax is one where poorer people pay a higher proportion of their income in tax than do richer people. A **flat rate tax** is regressive because, as your income rises, the proportion paid in tax falls.

Summary

Public goods are those things that only the government can supply since private firms would have no incentive to do so; whereas merit goods can also be supplied by private firms, but the government intervenes to ensure that more people can use the good than would be the case if it were left to private firms.

Demerit goods (or economic bads) are things which the government wishes to put people off buying, either by banning them or by taxing them.

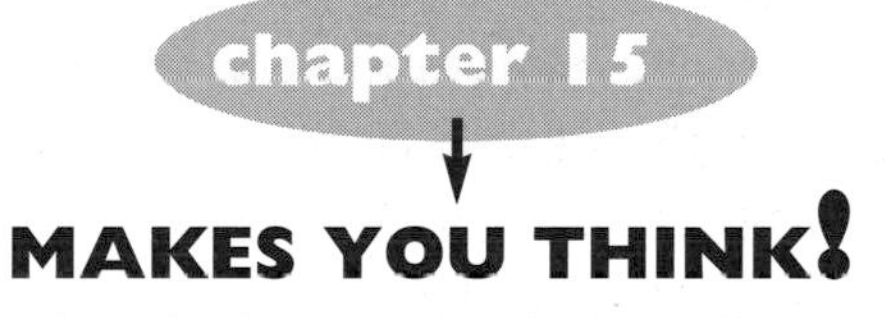

1 Decide whether each of the following are public goods, merit goods or demerit goods:
   (a) the ambulance service
   (b) Cheltenham Ladies College
   (c) tobacco
   (d) the RAF
   (e) refuse collection
2 Research the following:
   (a) What is the current basic rate of income tax?
   (b) What is the current rate of National Insurance?
   (c) How much can somebody earn before they start paying income tax?
3 Somebody earns £18,000 a year. Some of that is tax free, whilst the rest will be taxed at the base rate. National Insurance, however, is paid on all of it. How much tax is paid, and how much is left of the £18,000?

Chapter 16

Privatisation in the UK

From 1945 until 1979, many British industries were transferred from the private sector to the public sector. As we have seen, businesses in the private sector are owned by individuals (see Chapter 11), while public-sector businesses are owned by the government. Public-sector businesses are often known as 'nationalised industries', and they are under the control of the relevant cabinet minister in the government. For example, in the UK, the National Health Service is a nationalised industry, and the Secretary of State for Health is ultimately responsible for it. Likewise, the Post Office is part of the Secretary of State for Trade and Industry's responsibilities.

Although the UK policy of nationalisation was largely associated with Labour governments, Conservative governments from 1951 to 1964 and from 1970 to 1974 not only accepted the existence of most nationalised industries but actually nationalised more themselves – as in the case of British Leyland and Rolls-Royce.

The reasons for nationalisation were varied, but included the following:

- *Reducing costs:* it was thought that bringing together lots of small companies into one large enterprise would reduce costs through the benefits of economies of scale (see Chapter 10). For example, the coal industry comprised a series of independent mines throughout the country until the 1940s, and no one mine had the money for major investment
- *Improved management:* when the great names of the railway industry such as the Great Western and the LNER disappeared in 1947 to create that industry, these companies were on their last legs. Although the railway companies were regional monopolies, they were regarded as being poorly managed. The government could now recruit the best managers and put them in charge of a national network. However, the problem was that the government never paid British Rail management enough to attract the best managers
- *Control of monopolies:* the gas, electricity, railway and telecommunications industries all share two characteristics. First, they have been run in the public sector, and second they are monopolies. Many people believe that where it is impractical to have competition in an industry, the government should own that industry, set its prices and spend any of its profits for the public good
- *Political reasons:* the 1945 Labour government was committed to nationalising the coal industry because it was believed that the safety and well-being of coal-miners had hitherto been sacrificed to make private profit. The National Union of Mineworkers believed that the government would take better care of miners than did private companies. The government was also able to set a number of social objectives for industries, such as with the electricity industry where they chose to make electricity cheaper than a profit-making private sector company would have done
- *Saving businesses:* Rolls-Royce is an example of a company which had gone bankrupt in the 1970s but which the Conservative government of Edward Heath did not want to disappear. Relatively few jobs were at stake, but the name Rolls-Royce was a source of British pride which had to be saved. On the other hand, the threatened closure of British

Leyland, the only British mass producer of British cars, threatened not only prestige but also many thousands of jobs

In 1979, Margaret Thatcher became the UK Prime Minister, and her Conservative government adopted a policy of transferring nationalised industries from the public to the private sector. This process is part of what is called **privatisation**, but strictly speaking it is actually **denationalisation** – privatisation describes something much broader.

The meaning of privatisation

Privatisation describes the process of shifting the balance in the provision of services from the public to the private sector. In addition to the complete denationalisation of industries, it has taken the following forms:

- *The sale of public-sector property.* Most noticeably, local councils have been forced to sell council houses to the people who live in them. The longer that someone has lived in a council house, the cheaper it becomes for them to buy it. When the house is sold, the council receives the purchase price, but this is insufficient to build new property. In any case, central government has prevented local councils from spending this money, and as a result the number of council houses has decreased
- *Compulsory competitive tendering.* This means that services which have traditionally been provided by local councils, such as rubbish collection, now have to be allocated to the private firm that offers the service at the lowest price. Often, a private company will employ the people who used to work for the council, and in many instances it is the council's own workforce that won the contract. For example, in Colchester, local services are provided by Colchester Contract Services, a business owned by Colchester Borough Council. Cleaning and catering in hospitals and schools have also been **put out to tender**, and the question often asked 'Is cheapest best?' It can be argued, indeed, that standards of cleanliness and nutrition have fallen as a result of tendering
- *The sale of part of a nationalised industry.* Sometimes, certain parts of industries are seen as attractive to the private sector. For example, Sealink Ferries was originally part of British Rail. In 1984, although the government was not ready to denationalise British Rail – that would have to wait for another decade – they did sell off Sealink from British Rail
- *Deregulation.* This means the relaxing of rules governing who can do what. One of the best-known examples of deregulation is in bus routes where, until the early 1980s, bus companies were licensed to operate certain routes. This prevented competition and, so it was argued, kept fares high and service poor. Over the last decade, bus companies have had more freedom to operate where they choose. However, it can be argued that this has led to bus companies concentrating on racing with each other to provide services on more popular routes while people living in less populated areas, on the other hand, have seen their bus service decrease or disappear. This process is sometimes called 'cherry picking', and it has implications for the privatisation of British Rail

Companies privatised in the UK since 1979

1979 British Petroleum (only partly state-owned)
1981 British Aerospace
Cable and Wireless
Amersham International
1982 National Freight Corporation
Britoil
1983 British Rail Hotels (part of British Rail)
1984 Sealink Ferries (part of British Rail)
Jaguar Cars (part of British Leyland)
British Telecom
1986 British Gas
1987 British Airways
Rolls-Royce
Leyland Bus (part of British Leyland)
Leyland Trucks (part of British Leyland)
Royal Ordinance
British Airports Authority
1988 British Steel
British Leyland (sold to British Aerospace)
1989 British Water Authorities
1990 Electricity boards
1991 Electricity generation
1995 British Coal

Why privatise?

The privatisation programme of the Conservative government has had several objectives:

Reducing costs

Nationalised industries were seen as being inefficient. They made large losses that then had to be paid for out of taxes. This encouraged workers to be lazy, and there was also overmanning (or should that be 'overpersonning'?) since there was no incentive for managers to produce at a low cost. On the other hand, private-sector managers have every incentive to produce at as low a cost as possible, because otherwise they will lose their jobs.

The reason nationalised industries made large losses was often that the government told them to. As monopoly suppliers (see Chapters 13 and 17), they could charge what they liked, but in the 1970s they were told to adopt 'marginal cost pricing' – in other words, to charge a price that was equal to the extra cost of providing the service to that customer, rather than to charge a price high enough to cover the *average costs*. However, nationalised industries proved that they could easily make profits by putting their prices up before denationalisation and making large profits so that they were attractive to potential buyers.

Increasing choice and encouraging innovation

Public-sector businesses have no incentive to innovate, that is to come up with new ideas. In the private sector, on the other hand, businesses are continually trying to develop new ideas to beat the competition. It is certainly true that when British Telecom (BT) started to face competition in the supply of telephone equipment, new designs emerged and the country quickly switched from the slow dial to the push-button phone – this was a result of British Telecom losing its monopoly on the supply of equipment rather than of the change in the ownership of BT. Similarly, when ITV started in the 1950s and 1960s, the BBC reacted to the competition by significantly increasing the quality of its programmes – which it was able to do even while remaining in the public sector. However, many people are now worried that the proliferation of television channels will actually reduce choice, since it will not be worthwhile for companies faced with small market shares to produce good-quality television.

Improving quality

In the public sector, if customers are dissatisfied with the service they receive, they can complain, but there is still no incentive for the provider of the service to improve things. In the private sector, however, a business that fails to please its customers will go out of business. In the 1990s, the government tried to improve service in the public sector by introducing the 'Citizen's Charter'. This set out minimum standards of service that could be expected from businesses in the public sector. For example, if your train was more than an hour late, you would receive some compensation.

Economic freedom

In 1995, Michael Heseltine proposed the denationalisation of the Royal Mail. However, he was unable to go ahead because he found that several Conservative MPs thought that this would be 'a privatisation too far!' The Trade Secretary's argument was that, as a private company, the Royal Mail would be able to borrow money for investment and get involved in a wider range of business activities. However, many MPs argued that it was only the government's own rules that stopped the Royal Mail from doing those things now.

Wider share ownership

A major goal of the Conservative government has been to increase the number of people owning shares – they have sought to create, in their own words, 'a share-owning democracy'. Certain denationalisations have involved the heavy promotion of small allocations of shares to members of the public. Gas and electricity shares, for example, could be bought for relatively small amounts. Some of the thinking here was that workers who own shares would see themselves as capitalists rather than just workers, and might then be more interested in making profits rather than concentrating just on pay increases. However, most denationalisations have simply involved the government selling the public-sector business to an existing private-sector business; and even where members of the public have been encouraged to buy shares, within a year many of these shares have been bought up by financial institutions instead. Sixteen years after the policy of privatisation began, the proportion of the population that owns shares is only a little higher than it ever was.

Raising revenue

One important consequence of denationalising a business, particularly a very large one like gas, electricity or water, is that it raises billions of pounds for the government. This in turn has allowed the government to charge rates of tax that are lower than they otherwise would be.

The former Conservative Prime Minister Harold Macmillan, speaking as Lord Stockton a few years before his death, pointed to a problem with this policy. He described it as 'selling the family silver'. In other words, selling a valuable asset raises lots of money in the short term, but once it's sold it cannot be sold again, and yet the problem that led you to raise the money is still there.

Competition

The main argument that has been used to justify privatisation is that competition brings advantages: a business in competition must keep low prices and high standards of service in order to attract customers. However, although some denationalised businesses such as British

Airways or Sealink face very obvious competition, they also did *before* they were denationalised. British Telecom was denationalised in 1984, and at the same time Mercury was licensed to provide direct competition with British Telecom. Together, the two companies form a **duopoly** (i.e. where two companies dominate the market), but very few households have a Mercury 'phone: the fact that British Telecom already had most UK households connected to their network made it very difficult for a new entrant to compete.

Similarly, households in Plymouth do not have much of a choice as to whether they will buy their electricity from the South West Electricity Board or from Northern Electric. It would be impractical to have a series of switches in your house allowing you to choose the company from whom you will buy electricity, and it would be far too expensive for Northern Electric to transport power all the way down to a customer in Plymouth. Regional electricity companies, like the water companies, have a 'natural monopoly'.

Denationalisation has therefore done little to increase competition. Indeed, the government has recognised this by the appointment of regulators who have to approve the prices set by privatised monopolies – for example, OFWAT oversees the water industry, and OFTEL does the same for telecommunications.

Summary

Privatisation covers a range of policies aimed at increasing the private-sector provision of services while *reducing* public-sector provision. It is therefore the reverse of nationalisation, which is the transfer of businesses from the private to the public sector.

The government claims that privatisation increases efficiency, providing businesses with an incentive to keep costs down and standards of service high. The problem of natural monopolies has been addressed by the establishment of regulators.

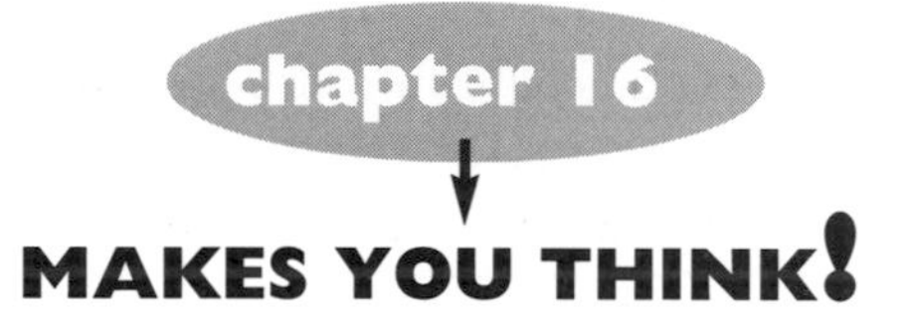

1 Of which type of privatisation is each of the following an example? Explain your answers.

   (a) the sale of British Rail
   (b) the use of Group 4 Security to transport prisoners to court
   (c) the sale of land owned by local councils
   (d) allowing other airlines to fly on routes once reserved for British Airways.

2 Does privatisation increase competition?

3 What should the state provide, in your view?

Chapter 17

Monopolies: good or bad?

In April 1995, Rupert Murdoch's world-wide News International Corporation offered large sums of money to the English Rugby League. On the one hand, this money was badly needed to finance ground improvements. On the other hand, this money was only to be made available if the best rugby league teams with 100 years of history and loyalty behind them merged into smaller numbers of teams to form a super league. From the rugby league supporters' point of view, the good news was that there would be new money available both to improve the quality of amenities at matches and to retain star players. The bad news was that there would be less choice of teams to support! In economics too, less competition may have both advantages and disadvantages.

The meaning of monopoly

An economist would define a **monopoly** as a single producer in an industry. However, the law of the UK defines a monopoly as any business controlling at least *one-third* of the market. Obviously, this legal definition is a loose one since 'mono-' means 'one' and yet under the law you could have *two* monopolies in the same industry. Indeed, in the washing-powder market, Unilever and Procter & Gamble dominate the market, so that from a legal point of view both these companies are monopolies, although an economist would here describe the situation as a **duopoly** ('duo-' meaning two). The essential point is that the law recognises that competition is generally better for consumers than a *lack* of competition. That is why if a proposed purchase of one business by another in the same industry will lead to one company controlling more than a third of the market, this proposed purchase must be investigated by the Monopolies and Mergers Commission (MMC). However, it is also recognised that monopolies can sometimes be 'in the public interest', and so the Secretary of State for Trade and Industry, acting on the advice of the MMC, must either agree to or reject a proposed takeover. In the case of very large businesses, or where a business based in more than one EU country is involved, the European Commission also has the power to stop a takeover.

From the late nineteenth century onwards, the USA has also attempted to curb monopolies. The government first sought through anti-trust laws to prevent the outright emergence of private monopolies in major industries by using the law and the courts to impose competition on firms in these industries. The American practice in the case of many natural monopolies (where economies of scale are so great that it would be impractical for a competitor to enter the market) – especially in the production and distribution of power, in public transport, and in communications – has been to allow private ownership but to control the prices charged and the extent of services through regulatory agencies such as the Interstate Commerce Commission, the Federal Communications Commission and the Federal Power Commission.

Monopoly power

Where a monopoly exists, the only limit on price is what consumers are willing to pay. Here, businesses do not have to worry about competitors, because there are none. However, the monopoly cannot just charge what it likes because if the price is too high, people will not buy their good or service. The monopoly therefore has to take note of the consumer's demand curve (see Chapter 4). In fact, a monopoly can set either the price it charges or the quantity that will be bought, but not both.

The monopoly will produce up to a level where the cost of producing one extra unit (i.e. the marginal cost) is equal to the money received from its sale (i.e. the marginal revenue) (see Chapter 9). This is because we assume that as production increases, two things happen: on the one hand, the costs of producing an extra unit start to rise, while on the other hand the extra revenue from producing extra units falls.

Look at Figure 17.1. The profit-maximising point at which to produce lies at the level of output where the MC curve crosses the MR curve. We then follow that line up to the average-revenue line – which is also the demand curve – to find the price at that level of output. This is the price which will be charged, and it is higher than the price that would be charged if there were competition. This is really because of the demand curve. If there were competition, the demand curve would be much more elastic (see Chapter 7) since in this case a price increase would lead to people switching to a different supplier. In a monopoly, however, all that people can do if the price is too high is give up consuming the product.

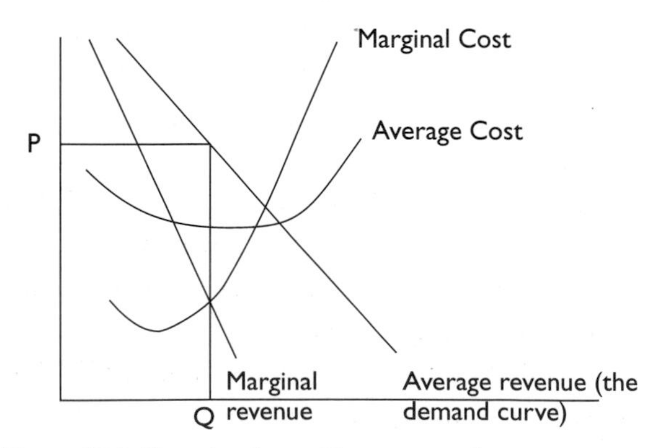

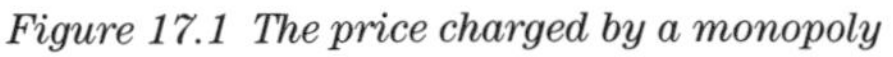
Figure 17.1 The price charged by a monopoly

Price discrimination

Why do 'phone companies charge higher prices for telephone calls made before 6 pm? Because *more* people want to make 'phone calls before 6 pm. This is an example of **price discrimination**: charging different groups of customers different amounts for the same product. This is done because in any market there will be some consumers who will be willing to pay more than others. Different groups are going to have different elasticities of demand for a product. People whose demand is inelastic – perhaps because they have to make calls during working hours, or (in the case of trains) because they have to travel at 'peak' times – will be prepared to pay a high price. On the other hand, a low price may attract people who could quite easily not make the 'phone call without Bob Hoskins (in recent advertisements) reminding them that 'It's good to talk!', or people whose travel is not essential.

Oligopoly

An **oligopoly** exists where a small group of companies dominate a market. Here – as for example in the petrol industry – it does not make sense for firms to compete on price: if British Petroleum (BP) were to announce a cut in its price, then Shell, Esso, Texaco and Q8 would quickly follow to avoid losing their customers to BP, and all that would happen is that all the companies would lose revenue. Similarly, if Shell were to try to *increase* its prices, many motorists might switch to the other companies instead. Shell could only get away with a price rise here if the others were to follow suit.

It would make sense for the companies in an oligopoly to all get together and agree to put their prices up at the same time. A group of companies that come together for this purpose is called a **cartel**, and these are very beneficial to producers. On the other hand, consumers would be forced to pay higher prices; and cartels are in fact illegal in the EU.

Figure 17.2 is known as the kinked demand curve, and it applies to oligopolies. It shows that the best thing for a business to do in an oligopoly is to keep its price where it already is. Above the existing price, the supply curve is elastic since customers would here switch to competitors. Below the existing price, the demand curve is inelastic since the quantity sold will not be increased by a price cut because the other companies will all be doing the same. Therefore, a higher or a lower price both result in less revenue.

As businesses in an oligopoly cannot compete on price, they instead try to create strong brand images, or they introduce schemes to encourage brand loyalty. in 1995, Tesco introduced its discount card whereby you were awarded points every time you spent a certain amount at Tesco.

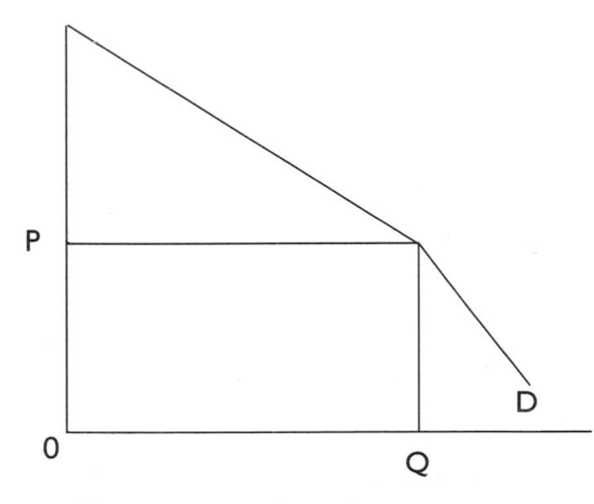

Figure 17.2 The kinked demand curve

Within a month, Sainsbury had launched a similar scheme. Many petrol stations offer tokens for you to collect towards gifts.

The benefits of a monopoly

It can be argued that, under certain conditions, a monopoly brings *benefits*. Often, indeed, the European Commission will rule that a monopoly is the best outcome because it will result in a better service to customers. For one thing, monopolies often have significant resources available for research and development which a number of smaller competing companies would not have. The arguments for a monopoly are very similar to those for nationalisation in Chapter 16. Many people would argue that there is a need for monopolies. People differ on whether these should be public-sector monopolies run by the state or private-sector monopolies regulated by the state. There is, however, general agreement on the need to control monopolies to protect the interest of consumers.

Summary

A monopoly can set either the price or the quantity supplied but not both. A monopoly that is trying to maximise profits will operate at the level of production where marginal cost equals marginal revenue.

Oligopolies exist in several markets, and they compete using **non-price competition**.

Monopolies can be beneficial to the economy in certain circumstances.

The European Commission and individual governments have a role in regulating monopolies.

chapter 17

MAKES YOU THINK!

1 How many natural monopolies can you think of? In each case, explain *why* what you have thought of is a natural monopoly.

2 Do the advantages of monopolies ever outweigh the disadvantages?

3 In the mid-1990s, there was a pattern of building societies merging and some being taken over by banks. Who were the gainers in this process, and were there any losers?

Chapter 18

The environment: are externalities a necessary evil?

In the middle of the 1980s, scientists and pressure groups began to convince governments that the **ozone layer** was being destroyed by groups of chemicals called **CFCs** (chlorofluorocarbons). In 1987, the most industrialised **developed countries** of the world signed the Montreal Protocol, committing themselves to phasing out the production of CFCs by the year 2000. Later, however, it was agreed to phase them out by 1996. CFCs destroy the ozone layer which protects the earth from the harmful effects of the sun's ultraviolet light.

NASA issues shock ozone warning

'Even if CFCs were phased out at once, it would take until 2060 or 2070 to restore the ozone layer to health – this legacy will be with us for a long time', Dr Kurylo said yesterday. Ozone depletion over the Antarctic is blamed for the blinding of sheep in southern Chile, where shepherds are now issued sunhats and dark glasses as protection against the barely filtered ultra-violet rays. Before the latest findings, the United Nations Environmental Programme warned that increased ultra-violet radiation could mean another 1.6 million cases of cataracts and another 300,000 of skin cancer in the world by 1999.

(The Guardian, 5 February 1992)

The ozone layer protects life on earth by shielding the planet from ultraviolet light that destroys living cells causing cancer and blindness. Scientists discovered that CFCs are the chemicals that destroy ozone. These chemicals were released into the atmosphere when used as a propellant for aerosol sprays, or as a coolant in fridges and freezers. The CFC problem was highlighted in the news, as was the fact that aerosols were a major contributor. Consumers quickly switched to buying aerosols that did not use CFCs, and as a result, manufacturers stopped making such cans. However, until 1992, CFC use in fridges and freezers remained constant because it proved difficult to find an alternative. Faced with the prospect of the 1996 ban, businesses switched to using HCFCs (hydrochlorofluorocarbons) for refrigeration units. The problem with HCFCs, however, is that they contribute to **global warming**.

The CFC problem is relatively easy to deal with in comparison to global warming – or the **greenhouse effect**, as it is often called. Carbon dioxide in the atmosphere is necessary to keep the Earth's surface temperature at around 15°C – about 30°C warmer than it would be if there were no carbon dioxide in the atmosphere. As more of the world becomes industrialised, the problem is that, as we pump more carbon dioxide into the atmosphere by burning fossil fuels such as oil, gas and coal, so the Earth's temperature rises. You may think that this is great because it means that we will have nicer weather. While this may be true, the changes in the weather pattern will also change the sort of food countries are able to grow. In addition, the deserts will expand (indeed this is already happening), leaving countries that are already on a knife edge as far as feeding themselves is concerned now unable to produce crops to either eat or sell. Furthermore, the icecaps of the Arctic and Antarctica will begin to melt, leading to a rise in the sea level around the world, and low-lying land (where many of the world's largest cities are found) will be flooded. All this will happen very slowly, so there is no need to panic, but we do have a big problem!

Cut in ozone could raise food prices

Scientists have backed up government fears that food prices will rise because increasing ultraviolet radiation in the atmosphere is expected to cut by one-fifth yields of vegetable crops such as peas, barley and oil-seed rape. Their research was funded because of the steady decrease in the protective ozone layer. It confirms some tree species, such as beech, will also be badly affected, a conference in London heard yesterday. The increased radiation cuts growth rates in some species and can cause trees to come into leaf early, leading to frost damage.

(The Guardian, 26 September 1992)

The meaning of externalities

An **externality** is something that occurs as a result of a production process but which will also affect people who are not involved in that process. A **negative externality** is an undesirable side-effect of any production, while a **positive externality** is a desirable side-effect. Pollution is the obvious example of a negative externality, but you also sometimes get positive externalities. For example, when a new hotel is built with a leisure complex, the leisure complex may be open to local residents and so they too enjoy the benefit of the hotel. In addition, local people may get jobs in the hotel, and so that is another positive externality.

In everyday English, people speak of social costs and social benefits. Economists use the same terms but slightly differently: what people in everyday English call a social cost the economist calls a negative externality, and a social benefit they call a positive externality. To an economist, social cost = private cost + externalities. Don't forget, however, that externalities, as already mentioned, can also be positive, in which case the social cost may be *less* than the private cost. Indeed, a positive externality such as fewer road accidents, for example, may so outweigh the private cost of building a new road that the government decides to do it. The big problem is attaching monetary values to externalities. How much is the value of an avoided fatal accident? How much is the value of a site of scientific interest that is to have a motorway built through it, such as in the case of the M3 motorway being extended through Twyford Down?

When private businesses are deciding whether to go ahead with a project, they will consider whether the private benefits outweigh the private costs. Similarly, when governments make decisions, they take into account whether the social benefits outweigh the social costs. This is called a **cost–benefit analysis**.

Examine the following information on a proposal for a project to be undertaken by a private-sector business:

Public transport in Newtown: proposal to build a tram line

Cost of building tram lines	£10 million
Cost of buying trams	£5 million
Cost of building tram stops	£1 million
Cost of providing ticket machines	£500,000
Wages over 10 years	£10 million
Projected income over 10 years	£17 million

(The figures are calculated in today's prices. In other words, the income over 10 years will be more than £17 million because of price rises, but it will probably be the equivalent of £17 million today.)

Does the benefit outweigh the cost? Would you go ahead with the project? As a local authority, what additional costs and benefits would you take into account before deciding whether the social benefit of this project outweighs the social cost?

Policies for reducing externalities

One way for a government to reduce externalities is to simply ban them – as with CFCs. However, this is not always practical as the production process may result in something that is in great demand, and because alternative technology may need to be developed. The government can help to persuade businesses to develop alternative technology by applying the 'the polluter must pay' principle. Here, the government can ensure that the business contributes to the cost of cleaning up any pollution by putting a tax on the product. This will make the product more expensive than it otherwise would be, and so less will be bought. There will also, as a result, be an incentive for businesses to develop an alternative way of producing the product without pollution so that they can avoid the tax, sell their product more cheaply and so capture customers from the competition. Including all the costs of production in the business's private costs is known as a **market-based solution**. Economists refer to this as **internalising the cost**. In other words, instead of pollution being an externality paid for by someone else (i.e. by the government from taxes), the cost now becomes a private cost that the business must include as a factor when deciding whether it is worthwhile producing something.

Using the tax system was very effective in helping to phase out leaded petrol. However, the problem still remains that many roads become congested by the volume of traffic using them, and the exhaust from cars is the major contributor to the carbon dioxide that causes global warming. An alternative to a market-based solution is a **regulatory solution** where the government imposes restrictions on economic activity.

Summary

Social costs comprise private costs plus externalities. Externalities can be reduced through a ban or by use of the tax system. Sometimes, consumer information and choice can make manufacturers change production methods – as in the case of aerosols.

A cost–benefit analysis is carried out by central or local government to assess *all* the costs and benefits involved in undertaking a project.

1 Explain, using a supply and demand diagram, why a cut in ozone could raise food prices.
2 What are the social costs of car ownership? Make a list of private costs and externalities. How can these costs be paid?
3 Here are some suggestions for reducing car use and traffic congestion. Which policies would you choose if you were the government, and how might they work?

(a) Increase the price of petrol by 50p a litre
(b) Increase car tax to £200 a year
(c) Introduce road pricing in city/town centres so that people have to pay a fee to use certain roads
(d) Introduce tolls on motorways
(e) Issue tags that could record a car's mileage, and charge a fee for each mile travelled
(f) Give a subsidy to the operators of trains and buses to make the fares cheaper

What would be the effects of any policy you have chosen? Who would lose out? What problems might there be?

Further reading

EBEA 16–19 Project (1995), *Core Economics*, Oxford: Heinemann.

Chapter 19

When should governments intervene in markets?

We saw in Chapter 16 that there has been a move towards 'freeing up markets' in Western countries over recent years. Since 1979, the Conservative government in the UK has attempted to move as much business activity as possible from the public sector to the private sector because it believes that 'markets work'. Sixteen years later, there were still activities that had to be carried on by the government. We saw in Chapter 15 that in any country, the government will have to provide 'public goods', and that just what else the government is involved in is then a political choice. We have also seen that without government regulation, monopolies could exploit consumers and there would be no restrictions on pollution.

It is true that today the government in the UK intervenes in the economy far less than it did in the 1970s, but there are still many ways in which the government affects prices, incomes and the goods and services that can be produced.

The meaning of 'positive' and 'normative' economics

The title of this chapter asks a question that includes the word 'should'. This is not, therefore, a question that an *economist* can answer because the word 'should' implies a moral judgement. Economics can point to the consequences and effects of such judgements, but it is up to those individuals who are armed with the information and understanding gained from reading this book to answer the *political* question 'When should governments intervene in markets?' If we make the statement 'Governments intervene in markets', we can show that this is true; and such a statement we call a **positive** statement. If, however, we introduce the word 'should' and say 'Governments should intervene in markets', we have changed the statement to one which is **normative**. Strictly speaking, normative statements are for politicians rather than economists, but of course economists do have political opinions also. For example, the most famous and influential British (and possibly world) economist of the twentieth century (Keynes) was a member of the Liberal Party. His starting point for the intervention of the concept of **aggregate demand** and the structure of **macroeconomics** (see Chapter 21 onwards) was his passionate belief that unemployment is a bad thing. This indeed is why economists disagree: depending on their political view of the world, they will make different assumptions about how people behave, and about the relative importance of different economic problems. At a very simple level, right-wing economists believe that the best way to reduce unemployment is to reduce pay so that workers become more affordable for firms. On the other hand, left-wing economists believe that the best way to reduce unemployment is for the government to spend more on training, and on projects such as new schools and hospitals that will require extra people to work. Both sides can pick out economic theory, and indeed real-world statistics, to prove their point.

The Common Agricultural Policy (CAP)

Perhaps the main way in which most of us are affected by government intervention in the economy is through the **Common Agricultural Policy** (CAP), because this makes our food more expensive than it otherwise would be. The CAP was developed because after World War II, European governments were worried that Western Europe relied too heavily on food imports: during the war, both sides had suffered from food shortages since cheap supplies of food had to be shipped in from overseas. The founding countries of the European Community (now the European Union (EU) – see Chapter 28) decided that they needed a system to encourage farmers first to stay in agriculture (rather than continue the historic trend towards taking better jobs in towns) and second to increase production. As a result, all the members of the European Union agreed to the CAP, which is run by the European Union's central authority in Brussels and works as follows.

The Common Agricultural Policy is a way of influencing agricultural production. Each year, a guaranteed minimum price is set for a range of farm products, e.g. beef, olive oil, wine, apples, and butter. If the market equilibrium price (see Chapter 6) is above that minimum price, then the market operates in the normal way. However, in many countries, such as France and Germany, farmers can play an important role at elections, and so politicians are under pressure to raise the minimum guaranteed price each year so that it lies *above* the equilibrium price – see Figure 19.1. At this higher-than-equilibrium price, consumers demand a smaller quantity whilst producers, however, supply a *greater* quantity. In a free market, the price would fall to the equilibrium point and the producers would cut back production. However, the point of the CAP was to encourage farmers to increase production by guaranteeing them a price that made it worthwhile for them to produce more. The EU, therefore, steps in and buys up any excess production that results from the high price so that farmers do not cut their price to sell off stock.

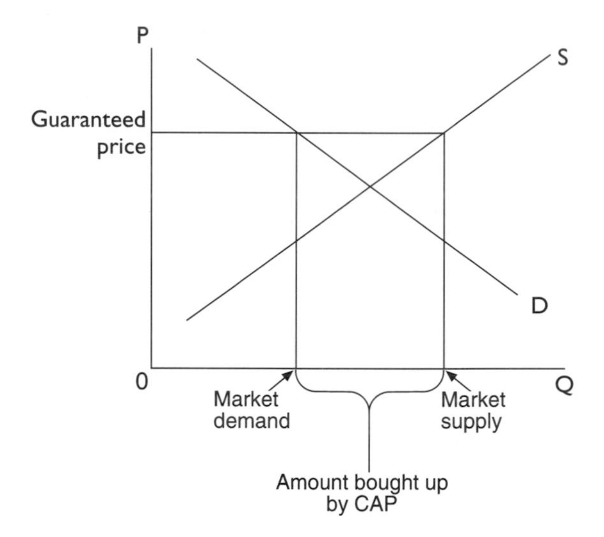

Figure 19.1 The CAP and the guaranteed price

In the past, indeed, the EU has bought huge amounts of excess agricultural products, and the name given to this process is **intervention buying**. In theory, the products are stored, and could be introduced back into the market if there were a particularly bad harvest one year, so that prices would be kept stable. In reality, however, this has never happened, and these great surpluses have become known as the 'wine lake' and the 'butter mountain'.

In the 1990s, the CAP policy has been modified to introduce **quotas**. Now, a minimum price is still guaranteed, but a farmer is only allowed to produce up to a certain quantity – i.e. their 'quota'. If a farmer produces more milk than their quota permits, they must pour it down the drain, or find some other use for it. One farmer decided to protest against this waste by offering people the chance to take a bath in his milk. This allowed the customer to be asked: 'Do you want it pasteurised, or just up to your shoulders?'

The result of the CAP is that producers have a guaranteed income each year. Farmers often complain that this income is not enough, but there are very few businesses that have such a guaranteed income. Consumers pay for this in two ways: first, by being charged more than the equilibrium price; and second, through taxes being used to buy up the extra supply and pay for the storage.

In the 1990s, there have been attempts to cut the over-supply of certain products by encouraging farmers to stop producing so much. 'Set-aside' is a scheme where farmers are paid money to not grow crops on some of their land. There are also payments (in the form of subsidies) for uprooting apple orchards so that fewer apples are produced. These are all ways of trying to affect the quantity produced without letting prices fall.

Agricultural products that are not stored and cannot be sold at the guaranteed price are destroyed. Can destroying food be justified when there is hunger in the world? What has economics to say about this?

The market for homes

For some years, the UK has had the problem that there are not enough homes for people who need somewhere to live. For most of the twentieth century, local councils have had the responsibility to house people who could not buy their own house. The Conservative government from 1979 onwards believed that housing should be in the private rather than the public sector.

There are few people who are able to rent out a property for someone else to live in. This means that the property that is available is in short supply but in great demand, and this leads to very high prices being charged. Is it right therefore to introduce **rent controls** making rents cheaper than they otherwise would be? Such rent control reduces the rent to below the equilibrium price (see Figure 19.2). This makes properties more affordable. However, at the same time, landlords find that because they will now get less rent, it is less worthwhile supplying property. So the effect of a rent control is that more people can afford the rents charged but

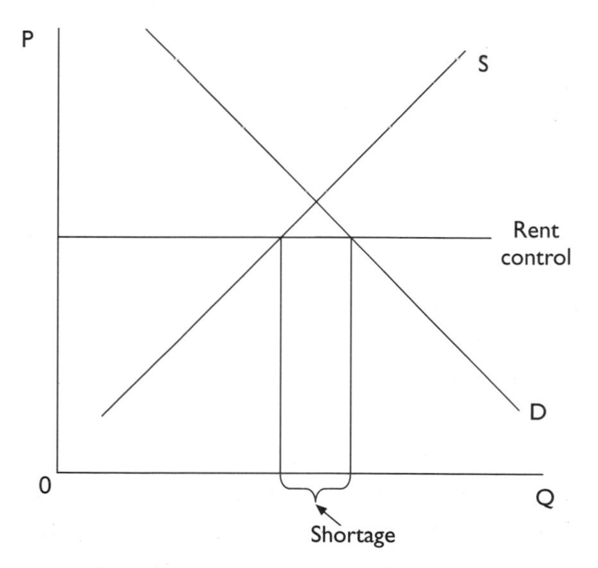

Figure 19.2 Rent control and the equilibrium price

that fewer places are available to rent. Does this make the problem better or worse? What do you think?

In addition, from 1979, people have been encouraged to buy their own home rather than to rent. In European terms, this is a British obsession: in the UK it has become quite normal for people to take out a mortgage and eventually own their own home, whilst in other countries (e.g. Germany) this is quite rare. To encourage people to buy their own home, there was a policy in the UK for many years (this extends back to well before 1979) that people received help from the government. The mortgage repayments were considered to be something desirable, a sort of merit good. Thus, governments decided that the part of people's income which they used to pay the interest on their mortgage should not be taxed: people could now claim back the tax here, and so their mortgage repayments were effectively being subsidised by the government. Since the 1980s, however, this subsidy has gradually been reduced, and by the time you read this book, it may have disappeared altogether.

Why has a government whose political aim was to encourage people to buy their own home withdrawn a subsidy to help them to do it? Well, look at Figure 19.3. As a result of Mortgage Interest Tax Relief (the MIRAS scheme) or a mortgage subsidy, buyers of houses can afford to pay more for their houses, just as if they had an increase in their incomes (see Chapters 4 and 6). However, the supply of houses is relatively fixed (i.e. there is limited scope for building more houses). The effect of the subsidy is to increase the price of houses, but it does not encourage many extra houses to be supplied, because most houses are bought from people who are looking to move to another house.

Other subsidies

From time to time, various goods have been subsidised to make them cheaper than they otherwise would be. Mortgage Interest Tax Relief is an example of a subsidy to the consumer which results in the price going up. In the late 1970s, basic foods such as bread were subsidised. In this case, the subsidy was given to the *producer* to make the produce cheaper than it otherwise would have been. A producer subsidy shifts the supply curve to the right, causing the price to fall and the quantity bought to increase – see Figure 19.4.

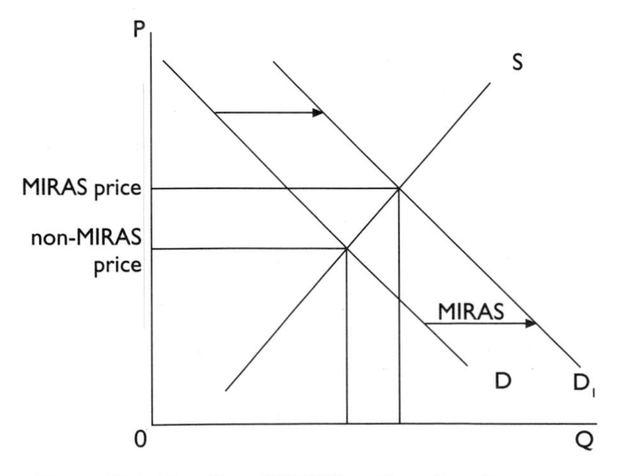

Figure 19.3 The effect of MIRAS on the price of houses

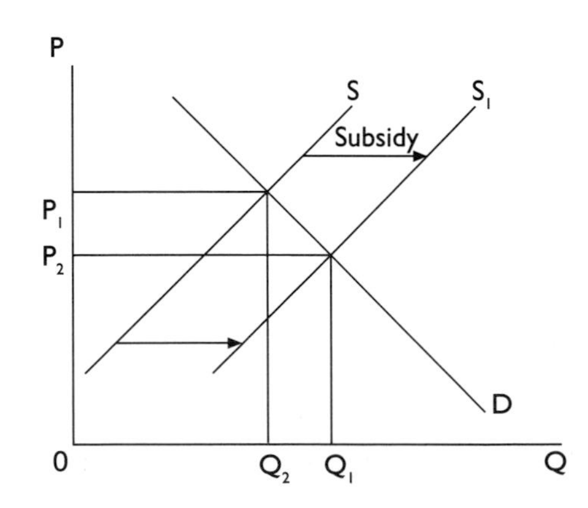

Figure 19.4 The effect of subsidies to producers on the price and the quantity demand of a good

Indirect taxes

Indirect taxes, such as value-added tax (VAT), are taxes on spending. In addition to being an important source of tax revenue for the government, they can be used to influence consumer behaviour. Food, children's-size clothes, books, newspapers and public transport (as already mentioned) are all zero-rated for value-added tax (VAT) in the UK. In other words, the government takes the view that people should be encouraged to buy these items, and so no VAT is charged on them. Other goods and services, however, have VAT of 17.5% (correct in 1996) charged on them. The rate of VAT and the range of goods on which it is charged vary in each EU country.

The government can thus decide to take tax *off* things where it wants to encourage consumption and to *add on* tax where it wants to *discourage* consumption. Cigarettes are the obvious example, where most of the price of a packet of cigarettes goes as tax to the government. There is an economic argument for this in that smokers cost the country more: they are much more likely to be off work sick than are non-smokers, they are likely to need medical treatment for long-term terminal illnesses, and they make non-smokers buy more washing liquid to get the smell of cigarette smoke out of their clothes! The switch to unleaded petrol by most cars in the late 1980s began when the then Chancellor of the Exchequer made the tax on leaded petrol higher than that for unleaded. This is one of the best examples of the government using the tax system to influence consumer behaviour.

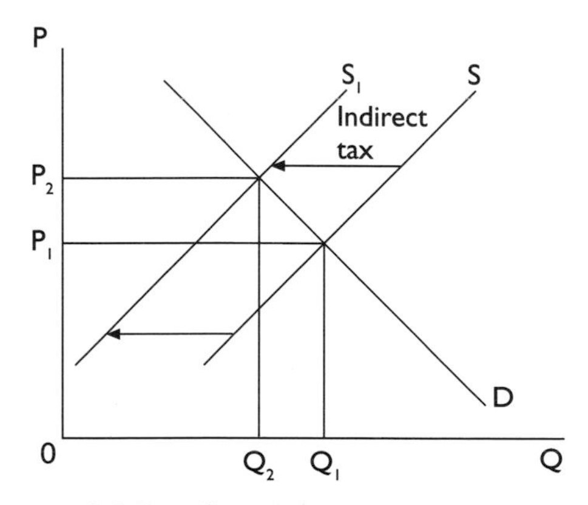

Figure 19.5 The effect of an indirect tax on the price and the quantity demanded of a good

Figure 19.5 shows that an indirect tax shifts the supply curve to the left, making the price higher and reducing the quantity consumed. Of course, the effect of the tax will depend on the elasticity of demand (see Chapter 7) for the product. Unleaded petrol provided a close substitute for leaded, but there are no obvious close nicotine substitutes for nicotine-dependent tobacco addicts.

Summary

Governments intervene in markets to regulate monopolies, to limit pollution, to encourage the consumption of socially desirable (merit) goods and services, and to discourage the use of socially undesirable (demerit) goods and services.

Governments intervene by using the following methods:

Intervention method	Effect on price	Effect on quantity bought
Guaranteed minimum price	Increase	Decrease
Consumer subsidy	Increase	Increase
Producer subsidy	Decrease	Increase
Indirect tax	Increase	Decrease

MAKES YOU THINK!

1 Explain in your own words why the EU pays farmers for 'set-aside'.

2 Does the government have a responsibility to the homeless, and if so how might they be helped?

3 In what ways might you use indirect taxes to influence consumer behaviour if you were the Chancellor of the Exchequer?

Part III

The national and international economy

Demand, supply and the circular flow of income

As with many Western countries (Germany and Austria being notable exceptions), the economic story of the UK since World War II has been described as **stop–go** or **boom and bust** economics. Very simply, both Labour and Conservative governments have tried to achieve both low inflation and low unemployment. Inflation and unemployment are both unpopular, but the problem has been that whenever a government has tried to decrease unemployment, it has increased the general level of demand for goods and services in the economy, and this has led to inflation. On the other hand, attempts to reduce inflation have involved reducing the general level of demand, and this has caused unemployment. (See Chapters 21 and 22.)

The 1980s began with a **recession** as the government tried to bring down inflation. A recession describes the situation where a country's output and income are both falling. It is defined as six consecutive months of falling national income. Midway through the 1980s, the then Chancellor of the Exchequer, Nigel Lawson, thought that he had beaten inflation and so began to reduce interest rates so that people with mortgages and loans had more money to spend. The result was a fall in unemployment and a rise in inflation. Faced with an inflation rate in 1990 of nearly 10% (higher than when the government came to office in 1979 with the control of inflation as its main target), interest rates were raised, and by 1993 the inflation rate was below 2% but unemployment was now up to 10%. This is what is meant by stop–go economics.

The meaning of aggregate demand

Aggregate demand is all the different demands for goods and services added together. Most of this demand comes from consumers, and this is called **consumption**, but firms also demand goods to help in the production process, and this is called **investment**. Furthermore, the government is itself an important purchaser of goods and services, and so we must also include **government spending** on the wages of government employees, the running costs of things like hospitals, welfare benefits, and the costs of new projects like roads or prisons. Finally, people living abroad may also demand things, and so we also include the difference between **exports** and **imports**. Aggregate demand comprises C (consumption) + I (investment) + G (government spending) + (X − M) (exports minus imports), or C + I + G + (X − M).

The circular flow of income

The **circular flow of income** is a model of the economy. Economists use **models** to draw a simplified picture of the way the economy works. By making it very simple, we can illustrate how certain things affect other things.

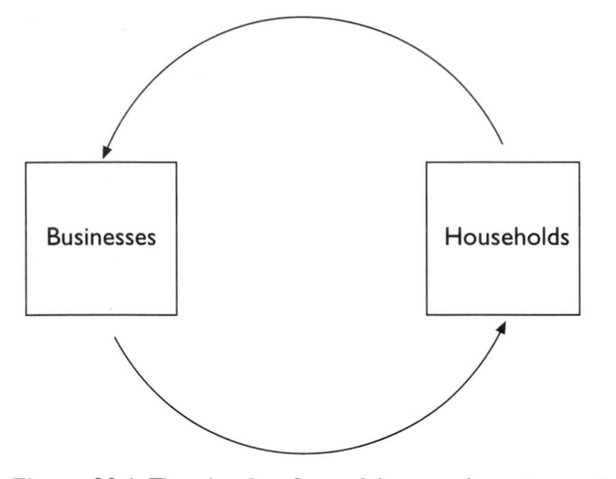

Figure 20.1 The circular flow of income in a two-sector economy

A simple two-sector economy with no government and no foreign trade would look as shown in Figure 20.1. In this model, for an economic system to exist we must have households and businesses. People live in households, and their role in the economy has two parts. First, according to this model, the factors of production (land, labour, capital and enterprise) are all owned by households (see Chapter 8). Businesses hire these factors of production in exchange for a reward (rent, wages, interest and profit respectively). Since *labour* is what most households can offer, the reward for this (i.e. wages) will not be very high unless there is something special about that labour (a high level of skill, a willingness to do dangerous or unpleasant work, or a high level of qualification). On the other hand, the owners of land, capital and enterprise are much more scarce, and so these people can become very rich because their services are in relatively short supply.

Households earn their money from businesses, and so there is a flow of income from businesses to households. But from where do businesses get their money to pay the households? Well, the second job of households is to buy up the output of businesses, so that there is also a flow of income from households to businesses. Businesses thus rely on households for their income just as households rely on businesses, and the economy is always in balance (or in 'equilibrium') because the income flowing from households to businesses is always equal to the income flowing from businesses to households.

Note that in this very simple model, households must spend all of their income on the output of businesses. There is nothing else they can do with it, because we have not given them the option of **saving**. This is clearly unrealistic, so we can make our model a little nearer the real world by adding a financial or banking sector where households can save. Any income that is saved will not then be spent on goods and services produced by firms, so firms will now have less income to pay for the hire of the factors of production. However, businesses now have the option of borrowing for *investment*. Indeed, banks want people to save with them so that they can then use that money to lend to people at high rates of interest. Now, note that if businesses borrow, for investment, a *greater* amount than households save (which can occur in the short term), then overall, the amount of money flowing around the circular flow will *increase*. On the other hand, if businesses invest *less* than

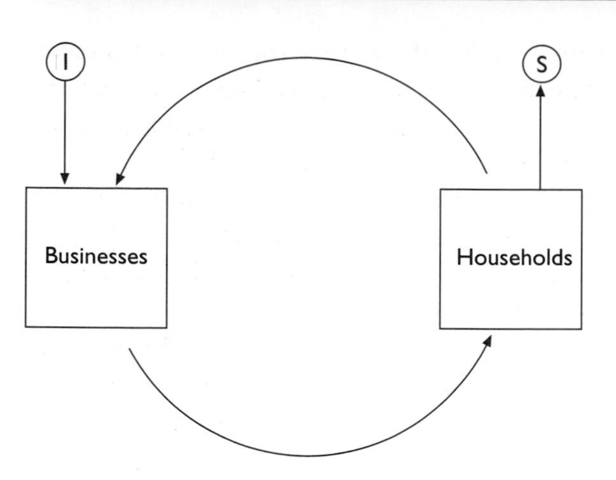

Figure 20.2 The circular flow of income with saving and investment added

people save, then the money in the circular flow will *decrease*. Or if, indeed (but this is most unlikely), savings *equals* investment, then the economy is in equilibrium. (See Figure 20.2.)

Injections and withdrawals

We now have an opportunity for extra money to *enter* the circular flow of income in the form of investment. Similarly, money can *leave* the circular flow through savings. Any money entering the circular flow is called an **injection**, whilst money leaving is known as a **leakage** or **withdrawal**. The principle has thus been set out that if the withdrawals (savings) equal the injections (investment), the economy is in equilibrium. In a real economy, however, savings and investment (the financial sector) are not the only ways in which income can enter or leave the circular flow. There are two other sectors: the government and foreign trade.

When people are taxed, their spending power is reduced. Therefore, not all of their income will return to businesses: some of their income will go instead to the government. Thus, taxation is a withdrawal. On the other hand, government spending is an injection.

Much of what we buy is not made by businesses in our own country, and the money to pay for these imports goes to businesses abroad who use it to pay for the factors of production in their own economy. Thus, although the goods are coming into this country, the money to pay for them is flowing out, and so imports are a withdrawal. Similarly, when foreigners buy goods from this country, the money to pay for these exports flows into our businesses, and so exports are an injection.

The economy is thus in equilibrium when all injections, added together, are equal to all withdrawals added together (See now Figure 20.3.)

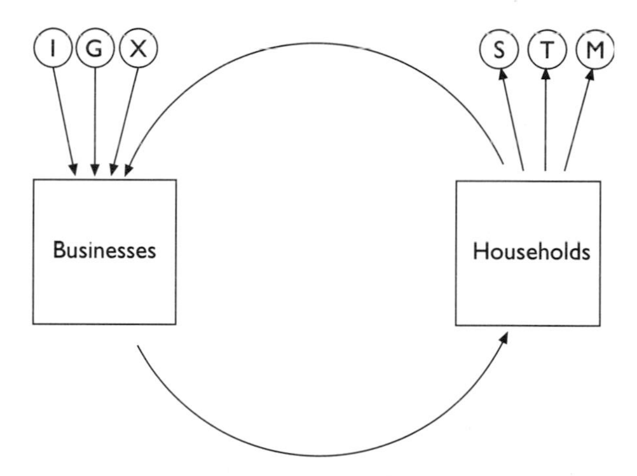

Figure 20.3 The circular flow of income with all injections and leakages added

These are the standard abbreviations used by economists:

Injections:

I Investment
G Government spending
X Exports

Leakages/withdrawals:

S Saving
T Taxes
M Imports

The consumption function

There is a certain amount of consumption that people must carry out to survive. Even if their income is very low and they are unable to save, people will need to buy certain things; and they will probably draw on past savings or borrow to do this – in other words, they will **dissave**. As their income rises, however, people will need to dissave less, and eventually they will reach a point where they can afford to start *saving* some of their income. The point where spending is exactly equal to income, so that there is neither saving or dissaving, is again called 'equilibrium'.

The essential point of the **consumption function** is that as people's income rises, they tend to spend a *smaller* proportion of it on consumption: an increasing proportion will be saved, and in addition, more income will be taxed and probably used to buy imports.

The multiplier effect

Remember that the circular flow of income means that when any money is in the system, it will carry on flowing between households and businesses until it gradually disappears through leakages. This means that any extra money injected into the circular flow will also flow between households and businesses until it disappears through leakages. Just how quickly it disappears will be determined by the size of the leakages. If people save a large proportion of their income, the amount passed on through extra consumption will be less than if people *spend* all of their income. As a result, any injection into the circular flow of income will increase spending not just by the size of the injection but by several times the size of the injection. This is called the **multiplier effect** because any injection is multiplied.

The County of Suffolk does not have a university. Suppose the government decided to create a new university on a greenfield site on the edge of Ipswich. Consider how this would effect the local economy. First of all, the university would have to be built. This would create jobs for construction workers. The construction industry is very dependent on government spending. Spending money on a new construction project is a good way of ensuring a high multiplier effect because very little of the spending goes on imports. These construction workers will then spend their money in local shops and businesses. As a result, the owners of these shops and businesses will in turn have more money to spend. Then, after the building is complete, people will be employed in the university doing all sorts of jobs. Many of these people will be lecturers, and they are paid above the national average. These lecturers will move to the area, creating extra demand for houses (pulling up prices and possibly leading to new houses being built) and again spending money in shops and local businesses. The initial increase in spending by the government will thus be passed on, raising the spending of many individuals who are not directly being paid by the government. The same effect takes place whenever there is an injection into the circular flow of income.

Fiscal and monetary policy

This chapter has concentrated on aggregate demand only, but it must now be pointed out that an increase in demand without an accompanying increase in supply will lead to higher prices. This is explained in more detail in Chapter 21. Very simply, when demand for a given good rises but businesses are unable to increase supply, the price goes up to ration who gets the limited supply of the good. Similarly, if *aggregate* demand increases and the country's ability to supply the goods and services demanded cannot keep up, then average prices will rise, and this is **inflation**. It is a relatively simple task for the government to control inflation: it can simply reduce aggregate demand by using either **fiscal** or **monetary** policy.

Fiscal policy uses taxes and government spending to regulate the economy at the time of the Budget. To reduce aggregate demand, either taxes can be raised or government spending can be reduced. If the aim is to stop prices from rising, then it would be silly to raise taxes on spending (such as VAT), so it is generally income tax that is raised. Increasing taxes or cutting government expenditure on major items is, however, politically unpopular.

Monetary policy involves the Chancellor of the Exchequer or finance minister telling the central bank (the Bank of England in the UK) to raise interest rates. However, in many countries, the central bank is independent of the government. To a great extent, this is indeed the case in the USA, where the Federal Reserve takes the decisions regarding interest-rate policy. In Germany, similarly, the Bundesbank is very independent, and the government can be frustrated in its wishes by the Bundesbank Council. At any rate, if interest rates do go up, then people will borrow less and save more, and this will leave less money available for consumption and investment. This too is politically unpopular as it makes people worse off; indeed, some people, as a result, will be unable to keep up their mortgage repayments, and some businesses in turn will be unable to repay their bank loans.

The problem with both these policies is that by reducing the demand for goods and services, they have the knock-on effect of reducing the need for workers. (The demand for labour is known as a **derived demand** because it is based on another form of demand – namely for goods and services.) Thus, reducing aggregate demand leads to unemployment. If reducing unemployment is a priority, then policies to *increase* aggregate demand will therefore have to be used: hence, with fiscal policy, taxes can be cut or government expenditure can be increased, and with monetary policy, interest rates can be reduced, making it easier to borrow and less attractive to save.

Aggregate demand and supply

In Chapters 4, 5 and 6, we saw that the working together of supply and demand in any market will affect both prices and the quantity produced (output). When we add up all the different demands for goods and services in a country, we arrive at aggregate demand, and adding up all the goods and services produced in turn gives us **aggregate supply**. We can then analyse aggregate demand and aggregate supply in order to study both **aggregate prices** (i.e. the general level of prices rather than the price of one good) and the general level of output (rather than the quantity produced of one good).

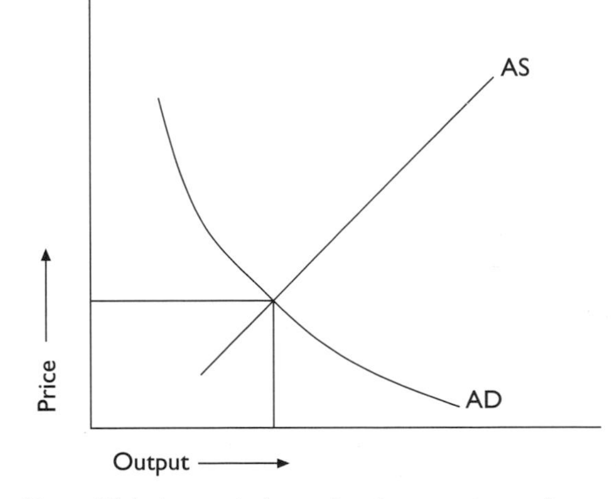

Figure 20.4 Aggregate demand and aggregate supply

In the aggregate demand and supply diagram shown in Figure 20.4, the vertical (P) axis measures the aggregate price level. This is sometimes called the **GDP deflator**.

> **Wise men play down tax rise threat**
>
> **The GDP deflator, which measures inflation, was 3.5 per cent in 1993 against 1992, the lowest since 1968.**

(The Times, 23 February 1994)

The horizontal axis measures aggregate output, which could also be called **real GDP**. GDP stands for **gross domestic product**, and it is a measure of all the goods and services produced in a country.

The aggregate demand curve slopes downwards to the right just like demand curves for normal goods, and for very similar reasons: the amount of goods and services that any level of aggregate demand can buy will depend on the price level; lower prices mean that a greater quantity of goods and services can be afforded, whilst higher prices mean that a smaller quantity can be bought. Similarly, the aggregate supply curve slopes upwards for much the same reason as does the supply curve for a normal good: if all other things remain unchanged (i.e. wages, raw-material prices etc.), businesses will generally find it profitable to *expand* production when the aggregate price level rises.

At this point, you may well be thinking 'So what?' Who can blame you? When will I stop asking questions and get on with it? Okay, here we go!

Suppose the government decided to cut interest rates. This relaxation of monetary policy will lead to an increase in both investment and consumption as loans become cheaper and it becomes less attractive to save. This is shown in Figure 20.5, where the level of aggregate demand increases from AD to AD_1. Output increases from Y to Y_1, and the price level increases from P to P_1.

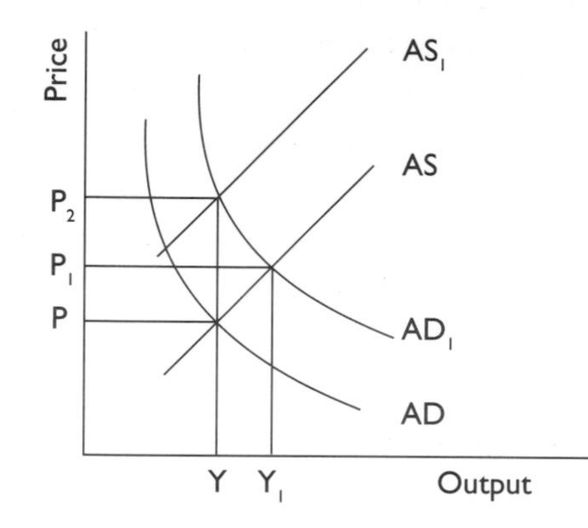

Figure 20.5 Changes in aggregate demand and aggregate supply as a result of a cut in interest rates

Now, as businesses and workers realise that the price of goods and services has increased, they will seek higher prices and wages too. These increases shift the aggregate supply curve to the left, from AS to AS_1. The original increase in output is eventually reversed, with the increase in aggregate demand leading to higher prices. There is equilibrium at the point where AS_1 crosses AD_1, with output back at its original level of Y and prices settled at P_2.

> **Business dismayed at interest rates rise**
>
> **The Chancellor's firm action to keep control of inflation by raising interest rates yesterday won the approval of the financial markets, but was greeted with dismay by business leaders, industrialists and mortgage lenders.**

The second increase in borrowing costs this autumn provoked cries of betrayal and warnings that consumers, already hit by higher taxes and mortgage rates, would be reluctant to spend.

(The Times, 8 December 1994)

A rise in interest rates will have the reverse effect on the aggregate supply and demand curves.

Summary

Aggregate demand comprises all the consumption, investment and government spending, plus any difference between exports and imports, in a country. The circular flow of income is a model of ways in which money flows in and out of the economy.

Governments can affect the amount of spending in the economy by the use of injections (e.g. government spending) or leakages (e.g. taxes). The multiplier effect exaggerates the impact of injections and leakages.

Aggregate demand and aggregate supply interact in a similar way to ordinary demand and supply to affect the general level of prices and output.

chapter 20

MAKES YOU THINK!

1 Draw a circular flow diagram with just households and firms. Now, for each of the following situations, write the appropriate letter on the diagram, with an arrow indicating whether it is an injection or a leakage:

(a) a family depositing money in a building-society account
(b) the building of a new hospital by the National Health Service
(c) a business borrowing £3 million from a bank to build a new factory
(d) a family buying a BMW car made in Germany
(e) the purchase of concert tickets in London by a group of American tourists.

2 If your main economic problem were inflation, what policies would you advise for the government?

3 If your main economic problem were unemployment, what policies would you advise for the government?

Chapter 21

Inflation

Table 21.1 shows that throughout Europe inflation levels were relatively low during the 1960s. Although the general trend was for inflation to rise in the 1970s and fall in the 1980s, the phenomenon was particularly acute for the UK.

Table 21.1 The annual percentage rate of inflation (based on the domestic retail price index)

	Europe 12	FRG	UK	USA	Japan
1960	–	–	–	–	–
1961	–	2.6	3.8	1.1	5.7
1962	4.9	4.1	4.4	1.1	6.8
1963	4.7	2.9	1.4	1.4	8.5
1964	3.9	2.4	3.5	1.4	3.5
1965	4.3	3.2	5.4	1.4	6.8
1966	3.6	3.6	3.8	3.1	5.3
1967	3.5	1.5	2.5	2.6	3.7
1968	2.9	1.7	4.8	4.2	5.2
1969	4.2	1.9	5.1	5.6	5.5
1970	5.4	3.3	6.5	5.9	7.6
1971	6.8	5.4	9.7	4.2	6.5
1972	6.3	5.5	7.0	3.5	4.8
1973	9.0	7.0	9.1	6.2	11.7
1974	13.7	7.0	15.9	11.1	23.0
1975	14.2	5.9	24.1	8.9	11.8
1976	11.6	4.3	16.6	5.8	9.5
1977	12.5	3.7	15.9	6.4	8.1
1978	9.0	2.7	8.2	7.8	4.3
1979	10.8	4.1	13.4	11.2	3.7
1980	13.6	5.4	18.0	13.5	7.8
1981	12.1	6.3	11.7	10.3	4.8
1982	10.8	5.4	8.6	6.2	2.8
1983	8.4	3.2	4.7	3.2	1.8
1984	7.2	2.4	5.0	4.3	2.3
1985	6.2	2.2	6.0	3.5	2.0
1986	3.5	−0.1	3.4	1.9	0.6
1987	3.3	0.2	4.2	3.7	0.1
1988	3.5	1.3	4.9	4.1	0.7
1989	5.2	2.8	7.8	4.8	2.3
1990	5.7	2.7	9.4	5.4	3.1
1991	5.0	3.5	5.9	4.2	3.3

FRG = Federal Republic of Germany

(EuroStat)

The meaning of inflation

Inflation is a rise in the general level of prices such that, after a period of time, you need more money to buy the same amount of goods as before. This does not mean that *all* prices have to rise. If the inflation rate is 5%, then in general, prices over the last year have risen by 5%. However, some of these prices may have risen by 2% or not at all, whilst others may have risen by 20%. The 5% represents a sort of average, but this must be qualified.

A simple average of all prices is not useful, because for most people, the price of a Rolls-Royce car rising by 10% is not as important as the price of electricity rising by just 1%. Therefore, a measure has been devised which takes account of the relative importance of different prices. A survey is carried out at regular intervals to find out how people spend their money. In the UK, this is called the Family Expenditure Survey. This information is used to give **weightings** to the goods and services which are included in the **retail price index** (RPI). The RPI is measured each month by sending civil servants to a variety of shops all over the country. The researchers record the prices of the items in the RPI, and the results are compared with those for the previous month. The RPI change in a particular month is designed to show the change in the **cost of living** for a typical family.

If the RPI in a particular month is 3% higher than for that month the year before, then the annual rate of inflation is 3%. However, this does not mean that for any individual, their cost of living will have risen by 3%. It depends on the individual's pattern of spending.

Is inflation a problem?

We shall see later that policies used to reduce the rate of inflation include increasing interest rates or taxes. In view of the unpopularity of such measures, people often question the need to control inflation. There is indeed a range of opinions as to how important the control of inflation should be.

People argue that constantly changing prices are a great inconvenience. It is suggested that people on fixed incomes, such as pensioners, lose out, and this is true if the pension is not linked to the rate of inflation. In fact, state retirement pensions are adjusted each year in line with the RPI. People with savings may lose out, but not if they have a savings account where the rate of interest is greater than the inflation rate (i.e. a positive rate of interest).

The two problems of inflation that cannot be avoided, however, are as follows. First, you may have studied in history the problem of when inflation runs out of control (**hyperinflation**). Money then becomes virtually worthless – as happened in 1920s Germany (when it was cheaper to wallpaper the house in money than to buy the wallpaper) – and people will then look for alternatives to money: they will switch to swapping goods for other goods (and here the convenience of using money will be lost), or alternatively they may give up on their national currency and seek to use a foreign currency instead – as in 1990s Russia where the US **dollar** is more acceptable than the Russian **rouble**. In Russia the annual rate of inflation ran at 2,200% in 1992. This was bad, but it only represents 25–30% a month. Hyperinflation is in fact defined as 50% a month, and so Russia has a little way to go before it reaches the heights of some Latin American countries! Other hyperinflations occurred in the USA and France in the late 1700s; in the USSR and Austria after World War I; in Hungary, China and Greece after World War II; and in a few developing nations in recent years. Hyperinflation is often accompanied by political instability.

Second, there is the problem of loss of competitiveness. Even at relatively low levels of inflation, if prices in country A are rising more quickly than prices in country B, then eventually it will become cheaper for citizens of country A to buy their goods from country B, leading to unemployment in country A. The only way to avoid this situation would be if the exchange rate were to change (see Chapter 27).

Real prices and interest rates

As prices are continually rising, making comparisons between price levels in different years is very difficult. To get over this, economists use the expression **real prices**. For example, if a computer cost £1,000 in 1990 and £1,100 in 1993, then its price has risen by 10% in that period. However, if prices generally had risen by 12% in that period of time, then the computer is relatively cheaper in 1993 than it was in 1990, so that its real price has fallen.

Similarly, if interest rates are 6% but prices are rising at 4%, the extra spending power that the interest rate gives is only 2%, so the **real rate of interest** here is 2%.

The following inflation rates occurred in an imaginary country called Ruritania:

1985: 4%
1986: 5%
1987: 9%
1988: 8%
1989: 9%
1990: 6%

In which year did prices fall?

Although the inflation rate fell in 1988 and again in 1990, there was not one year in which prices fell. Prices simply rose less quickly in 1988 than in 1987 and less quickly in 1990 than in 1989, but they still went up by 8% and 6% respectively.

The causes of inflation

The simplest explanation of inflation is called **cost-push**. This means that an increase in costs are passed on to the consumer as higher prices. These cost increases could result from a rise in the price of something used in the production process, such as power or a raw material, or from either a rise in wages or a desire for increased profits. As wages are often a large component of a firm's costs, an increase in wages can lead to an increase in prices. If this happens on a wide scale, prices *generally* will rise and workers will find that their wages now buy less. They are then likely to seek further wage rises, and this will lead to yet more price increases. This is called a **wage–price spiral**.

However, inflation can still occur even without increases in costs. A second cause of inflation is called **demand-pull**. You will remember from Chapter 6 that prices are determined by the interaction of two things: supply (i.e. how much a producer is willing to produce for sale at a particular price) and demand (i.e. how much customers are willing to buy at a particular price). Remember that in Chapter 4 we saw that demand is constantly changing since people's tastes and preferences change and advertising affects the behaviour of consumers. An increase in people's incomes will lead to a greater demand for goods and services. When demand for a good or service increases and supply remains the same, the price of that good or service will increase. Similarly, if there is a rise in the demand for things generally, then there will be a general rise in prices; and this latter case is what we mean by demand-pull inflation. The theory of monetarism is a special case of demand-pull inflation. Monetarists argue that the amount of money in circulation is what determines the level of inflation. They believe that if the amount of money to spend increases whilst the number of things on which to spend it remains constant, then the average level of prices will rise. This is self-evidently true. However, the economy is never static. Therefore, inflation, for the monetarist, is caused by the increase in the money supply occurring at a faster rate than the increase in the production of goods and services.

Actually, there are considerable difficulties involved in measuring the money supply. In Economics, the terms M0, M1, M2, M3 etc. are not motorways. They are differing measures of the amount of money in circulation, ranging from just notes and coins (**narrow money**) to a measure that includes bank and savings accounts and credit-card balances (**broad money**). Choosing the correct measure became so complicated that UK governments abandoned their practice of deciding by how much the money supply should increase each year in the mid-1980s. They had never been able to get it right, because although the government can determine the issue of notes and coins, they cannot control the banking system effectively. This is because banks are free to lend, and if customers cannot borrow from banks in their own country, they will turn to either foreign banks or other lenders.

Cures for inflation

To control cost-push inflation, there is an obvious need to control costs. This is very difficult as many costs are outside the control of any country. For example, an increase in the price of imports used as raw materials will often lead to cost-push inflation. However, during the 1970s, governments did target *wages* as a cost that could be controlled. **Incomes policies** were now used to limit pay claims. These policies were usually successful for about two years. After that, workers tended to push for pay claims outside the range of the policy. In the UK, this led to the 1978–79 'Winter of Discontent'. If workers go on strike, an employer is faced with the same decision as if there were no incomes policy: to settle or to cease production. With a private business, a government may be able to impose financial or legal sanctions on any such business that contravenes a pay policy. However, in the public sector (i.e. with people employed by central or local government), a government may be faced by the collapse of essential services.

The cause of demand-pull inflation is an increase in general demand that is not matched by an increase in supply. The technical term for this general level of demand, as we have seen, is aggregate demand, and it is made up of all consumption (buying by individuals), investment (buying by firms) and government spending plus any surplus of exports over imports. If a government wishes to reduce this type of inflation, it must adopt policies which will reduce aggregate demand. As we saw in Chapter 20, there are two types of policy that will achieve this. One is known as fiscal policy (anything to do with changes in tax rates or government spending); and the second is called monetary policy (changes in interest rates which are carried out on the say-so of the Chancellor of the Exchequer in the UK, the Bundesbank Council in Germany or the Federal Reserve in the USA – it varies from country to country). Let us recap.

One example of fiscal policy involves raising income tax. Putting up income tax will leave people with less money to spend on goods and services, and this will reduce demand. Businesses will therefore be left with less money to invest in new equipment. This policy is unpopular, and may be politically problematic for a government elected on the promise to reduce taxes. Cutting government spending would also reduce the demand for goods and services, but again this will be unpopular with those groups especially affected by any such cuts.

How, then, might monetary policy work? Increasing interest rates has an effect on businesses in that they are now less likely to borrow money to invest since the interest payments will be greater, making the investment decision less profitable. However, the biggest effect is on consumption. Individuals would now be less likely to purchase large items for which they may need loans, and so demand will fall. The biggest impact is brought about by the fact that a very large number of households (especially in the UK and USA) have **mortgages**. When the interest rate rises, mortgage payers are faced with larger repayments each month. They are then left with less **disposable income** (that is, money to spend on goods and services). On the other hand, savers receive more interest, but they are likely to *keep* this in their accounts rather than spend it.

The effect of reducing aggregate demand is a reduction in the demand for goods and services, and a reduction in the number of firms and people needed to provide goods and services. The economy is then likely to go into a recession, with high levels of unemployment, as we shall see in the next chapter.

Why, then, the concern with inflation? From what you have read in this chapter, do you think that it is worth the fight? At what rate is inflation a concern?

Summary

Inflation is a persistent tendency for prices to rise. It may be caused by costs being too high (cost-push), or by there being too much demand (demand-pull) in the economy for business to meet. Government cures for inflation involve attempts to keep costs down or the reduction of aggregate demand, and both have undesirable consequences.

Inflation becomes a serious problem if people lose confidence in the currency, or if domestic levels of inflation are above average so that people switch to buying the products of other countries.

chapter 21

MAKES YOU THINK!

1 At the beginning of a year, you have £10 to spend. During that year, the rate of inflation is 5%. At the end of the year, how much money would you need to have the same spending power as you had at the beginning of the year?
2 The following inflation rates occurred in Ruritania. During which years did prices rise?
   - 1991: 7%
   - 1992: 8%
   - 1993: 5%
   - 1994: 3%
   - 1995: 1%
3 Explain the problems of hyperinflation.

Chapter 22

Unemployment

During the 1950s and 1960s, unemployment in the UK never rose above 500,000. Unemployment then started a steady rise during the 1970s, but even in 1980 it was commonly believed that no government could expect to be re-elected with unemployment at over 1 million. The 1983 British General Election, however, proved this wrong, and throughout the 1980s and into the 1990s, the British economy has experienced historically high levels of unemployment (see Table 22.1).

Table 22.1 Registered unemployed as a percentage of the civilian workforce in the UK, 1960–92

1960	**1.4**	**1977**	**5.1**
1961	**1.2**	**1978**	**5.0**
1962	**1.6**	**1979**	**4.5**
1963	**1.9**	**1980**	**5.5**
1964	**1.4**	**1981**	**8.8**
1965	**1.2**	**1982**	**10.1**
1966	**1.1**	**1983**	**11.0**
1967	**1.9**	**1984**	**11.0**
1968	**2.1**	**1985**	**11.4**
1969	**2.0**	**1986**	**11.4**
1970	**2.1**	**1987**	**10.4**
1971	**2.7**	**1988**	**8.5**
1972	**3.0**	**1989**	**7.1**
1973	**2.1**	**1990**	**6.4**
1974	**2.0**	**1991**	**8.4**
1975	**3.2**	**1992**	**9.8**
1976	**4.8**	**1993**	**9.7**

(Eurostat)

Some economists believe that the change from the low levels of unemployment in the 1950s to the much higher levels of the 1980s and 1990s was caused by a long-term problem with the supply of labour. Other economists believe that unemployment is a problem concerning the lack of competitiveness in British businesses, caused by too little investment in machinery and too little training and education for the workforce. At any rate, the problem of unemployment has affected most Western countries over the last two decades (see Figure 22.1).

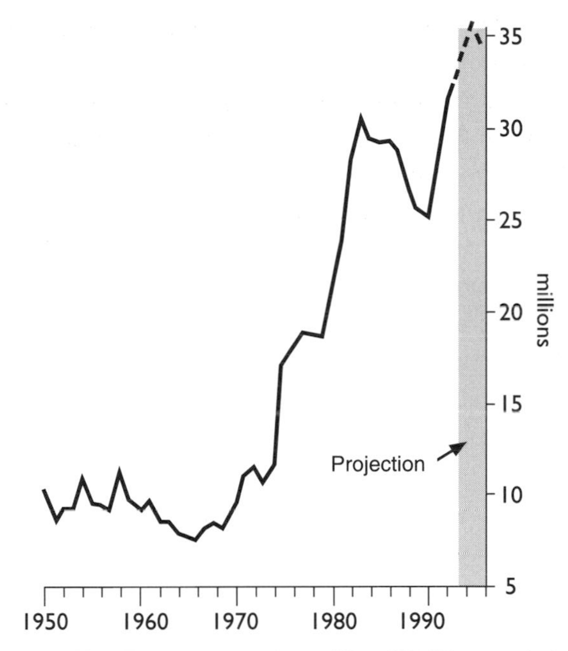

Figure 22.1 Unemployment in the West (OECD countries)

The meaning of unemployment

You may think that the meaning of unemployment is quite obvious, i.e. being without work. But think! Which of the following people, each of whom is without work, would you say is unemployed?

- Steve, aged 17, taking A levels at college and planning to go to university
- Jo, aged 19, training to be a doctor
- Emma, aged 24, looking after her 6-month-old baby

- Tom, aged 58, who has just accepted early retirement but would still like to work
- Martin, aged 68, who would like to work but is considered too old
- Suzanne, aged 28, who is desperately looking for a job and has to rely on her husband's income of £9,000

According to official UK government statistics, none of the above is unemployed. This is because the official UK government definition of unemployment is: people registered as seeking work and claiming benefit for being unemployed from the Department of Social Security (DSS). Both these conditions must be met. In economic theory, on the other hand, unemployment is considered to be: those people who are without a job but are prepared to accept one at existing wage rates. Some of the people above are clearly not seeking work. Tom, Martin and Suzanne, on the other hand, *are* all looking for work but are unable to claim unemployment benefit. Therefore, many people believe that official measures of unemployment are underestimates.

Types of unemployment

Economists distinguish between different types of unemployment in the following way. The first two – frictional and seasonal – are forms of unemployment that are always with us.

Frictional (or search) unemployment

Most workers who leave a job move quickly to a new one. This short-term unemployment is called **frictional**, and it existed even during the low unemployment levels of the 1950s and 1960s.

Seasonal unemployment

Some workers, such as those employed in tourism or in building, are only employed for part of the year. Such **seasonal unemployment** tends to rise in winter and fall in summer.

Next are some rather more worrying forms of unemployment, both because they indicate that there are weaknesses in the economy itself and because they have lasted longer and affected more people than was the case in the 1950s and 1960s.

Structural unemployment

Structural unemployment occurs when changes in the structure of employment come about. For example, the steel and the shipbuilding industries in the UK experienced rapid decline during the 1970s and 1980s, and many former steelworkers and shipbuilders became unemployed. Similarly, during the 1980s and 1990s, the coal industry has experienced a dramatic decline. Many villages were built as a result of the sinking of a coal mine, and so there is often no alternative employment available in the area. Structural unemployment has been present since the Industrial Revolution as new processes replace old. New industries need to employ people, but as these new industries may not set up in the area where the old industry existed, pockets of severe unemployment may remain. This leads to regional unemployment. Primary and secondary industries based in the north of the UK have been particularly affected, so that even during the 'boom' of the mid/late 1980s, unemployment in northern regions remained high.

Cyclical unemployment

Cyclical unemployment is brought about by a fall in aggregate demand. The history of the British economy has been one of increases in aggregate demand followed by decreases (see Table 22.2). Notice the pattern of booms and slumps. This pattern is what is known as 'stop–go' economics (see again Chapter 20).

Table 22.2 Percentage growth rates in gross domestic product at market prices in the UK, 1960–93

1960	–	1977	2.3
1961	3.3	1978	3.6
1962	1.0	1979	2.9
1963	3.9	1980	−2.2
1964	5.5	1981	−1.3
1965	2.5	1982	1.7
1966	1.9	1983	3.7
1967	2.3	1984	2.2
1968	4.1	1985	3.6
1969	2.1	1986	3.9
1970	2.3	1987	4.8
1971	2.0	1988	4.2
1972	3.5	1989	2.3
1973	7.3	1990	0.8
1974	−1.7	1991	−1.8
1975	−0.8	1992	2.0
1976	2.7	1993	2.8

(Eurostat)
Figures are at 1985 prices.

Cyclical unemployment falls when the level of aggregate demand increases, so the solution to this type of unemployment is relatively simple: increase aggregate demand. However, there are problems with increasing aggregate demand because it can lead to increases in inflation (see Chapter 21) or to a worsening in the **balance of payments** (see Chapter 25).

The costs of unemployment

Unemployment has some obvious costs for the individual. They will experience a fall in income, and so their standard of living will fall. In turn, this will reduce their family's ability to purchase what they want. The individual will also experience a loss of self-worth. People often describe themselves in terms of the job that they do, e.g. 'I'm an accountant', 'I'm a builder' or 'I'm a teacher'. Furthermore, being unemployed is very stressful, and the rate of suicides and ill-health of most kinds is markedly higher among the unemployed than among people in work.

There are also important costs to society arising from unemployment. Most obviously, the unemployed receive benefit which is paid for out of taxes. Therefore, either taxes have to be higher than they otherwise would be or government spending on other things has to be reduced. There is also a loss of government revenue, since the unemployed do not pay tax. At times of high unemployment, government spending rises whilst tax revenue falls, and as a result the Public Sector Borrowing Requirement (PSBR) increases to make up the difference; and the government now has to pay interest on this borrowing. And third, there is also a less obvious cost to society: that is the lost output that the unemployed would have produced if they had a job. If the unemployment rate is 10%, and the unemployed represent an average cross-section of the workforce, then perhaps if they were in work the country could increase its output by 10%. If this is so, then that lost output is the opportunity cost (see Chapter 2) of having unemployment.

Policies to reduce unemployment

The classical view of unemployment is that it is caused by the market for labour having more supply than demand. This can be illustrated by a demand and supply diagram. First, let's consider the market for tins of peaches. See Figure 22.2. The price of tins of peaches is higher than the equilibrium, or market clearing, price. This high price has caused too many tins of peaches to be

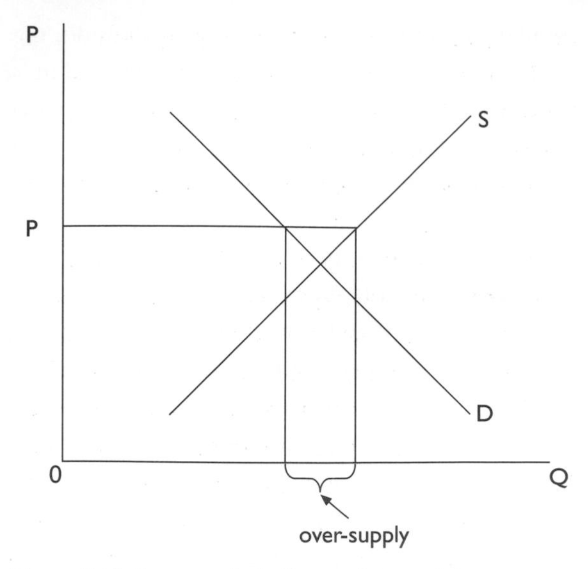

Figure 22.2 Over-supply in the peaches market

supplied by shops. Unable to sell at that price, large stocks of peach tins will thus build up until the price is cut. Classical economists believe that labour in turn has a market just like that for goods such as peaches – see Figure 22.3. If average wage rates are too high, firms will not take on as many new workers as there are workers seeking jobs. The difference between the number of people wanting to work at any wage rate and the number of workers that firms are willing to take on is the level of unemployment. According to this analysis, unemployment will

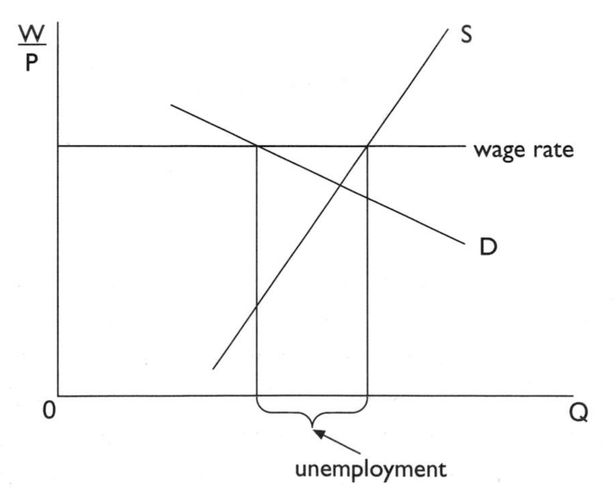

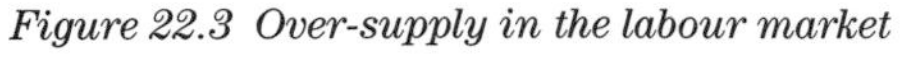
Figure 22.3 Over-supply in the labour market

be reduced by workers accepting jobs at lower wage rates. However, unlike tins of peaches, wages are downwardly sticky. In other words, contracts of employment make it difficult for firms to reduce the wage rate offered for a particular job when there are cheaper supplies of labour available.

Rate for the job

It makes you wonder. Recently I tried to get a cleaner in London and was told no one was available under £6.50 an hour for cash, or £7.50 an hour if I wanted to 'do it properly'. In South Derbyshire (unemployed 6.1 per cent and falling fast) both men and women would give their eye teeth for pay rates like that.

What happened to the willing army of unemployed in London? Have they priced themselves out of the market, or don't they really exist?

(A letter from the MP Edwina Currie, The Times, 30 November 1993)

The **Keynesian** approach to reducing unemployment (named after the economist John Maynard Keynes) has been to adopt policies aimed at increasing aggregate demand. Here, as already mentioned, the government should either increase government spending, reduce taxes or reduce interest rates.

The Chancellor of the Exchequer moved to crack down on inflation with a third interest rate rise in five months, yesterday. The move was met with almost universal

condemnation from both sides of industry, amid warnings that it would slow the pace of recovery. The interest rate rises come on top of tax increases that are still being implemented from last November's Budget.

Union leaders warned that the move would spark further insecurity in the labour market.

(The Guardian, 3 February 1995)

(How may the Chancellor's interest rate adjustments, as described in the above extract, affect the level of unemployment?)

However, other economists known as **supply siders** believe that policies to increase aggregate demand can only be successful for a short period of time, and are harmful in the long term because they lead to inflation. These economists believe in something called the **natural rate of unemployment**, defined as the proportion of the workforce that remains unemployed when the labour market is in equilibrium. In other words, various problems exist to prevent the unemployed from accepting jobs at the sort of wage rates where firms would be willing to take on more staff. These problems, and their appropriate solutions, are as follows:

Table 22.3 Supply side analysis

Problem	Proposed solution
High rates of income tax mean that people cannot afford to accept low-paid jobs	Reduce income tax
High levels of unemployment benefit mean that people cannot afford to take low-paid jobs	Reduce unemployment benefit
Trade unions force up wage rates and prevent firms from employing more workers at a lower wage rate	Reduce the effectiveness of trade unions
Workers lack the necessary skills to make it worthwhile for firms to employ them	Increase the skills of the unemployed

The natural rate of unemployment is more formally known as the **non-accelerating inflation rate of unemployment** (NAIRU). This is the level of unemployment which can be maintained without increasing the inflation rate.

Rather than use aggregate-demand increases to reduce the level of unemployment, the UK Conservative government since 1979 has tried to adopt the policies listed above. However, the data in Table 22.4 illustrates that actual reductions in unemployment have coincided with increases in aggregate demand, whilst increases in unemployment have been closely associated with falls in demand.

Table 22.4 A comparison of unemployment and GDP figures in the UK, 1979–93

	GDP percentage growth at market prices	Percentage of civilian workforce unemployed
1979	2.9	4.5
1980	−2.2	5.5
1981	−1.3	8.8
1982	1.7	10.1
1983	3.7	11.0
1984	2.2	11.0
1985	3.6	11.4
1986	3.9	11.4
1987	4.8	10.4
1988	4.2	8.5
1989	2.3	7.1
1990	0.8	6.4
1991	−1.8	8.4
1992	2.0	9.8
1993	2.8	–

(Eurostat)
Figures are at 1985 prices.

Summary

There is a range of views as to who should be counted as unemployed and therefore what constitutes the level of unemployment. Unemployment can be caused by too little aggregate demand in the economy; unemployment can be a supply problem, with workers unwilling or unable to accept jobs at the wage rates being offered; or unemployment can result from changes in the pattern of industry in an economy – e.g. the move from manufacturing to services.

The appropriate government policy will depend on the type of unemployment.

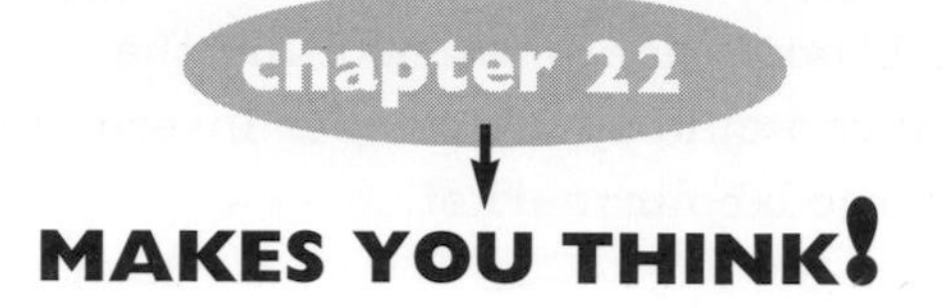

1 In this chapter, Edwina Curry MP suggests why there is unemployment in London. In your own words, explain her point.
2 Why might people be unwilling to work at £6.50 per hour?
3 Comment on the statement that 'a minimum wage has both negative and positive effects on unemployment'.

Further reading

Jay, P. (1994), 'In the grip of an age of fear', *The Times*, 10 October 1994, p. 17.

Chapter 23

Regional policy

Until the eighteenth century, the most prosperous parts of the UK, and indeed of any European country, coincided with the best agricultural land and areas around ports. Towards the end of the nineteenth century, the Industrial Revolution led to great shifts in wealth to the new manufacturing cities (Manchester, Birmingham, Bradford etc.). These industrial cities tend to be located in the North and the Midlands area of England, in South Wales and in central Scotland – see Figure 23.1). The Industrial Revolution was fuelled by steam, and steam needs two things: coal (to produce heat) and water. Large coal deposits and major rivers occur together in the areas indicated.

Figure 23.1 The concentration of industry after the Industrial Revolution

During the twentieth century, manufacturing industry has declined in importance as the economy has become more service-based. This has been reflected in a transfer of wealth from the North to the south of England where services are located.

The location of industry

As we have said, during the Industrial Revolution, a major force in deciding where a factory would be located was closeness not only to power but also to raw materials. Some raw materials had to be imported, and so those industrial areas of the north-east and north-west that were built near ports were ideal. However, with electricity now becoming the main source of power nationally, and with a good transport system of rail and road covering the country, these traditional reasons for location have declined in importance.

On the other hand, *markets* have played, and continue to play, an important role in where businesses locate, and being close to the market is particularly important for services: for example, people do not want to travel many miles to visit their solicitor. Traditionally, being located near your market has also been important for **bulk increasing industries**. These are industries where the transport cost of the finished product is more significant than the transport cost of the components necessary to make the product.

Also important to some industries may be a pool of skilled labour, and for this reason, businesses often set up where their industry already exists. For example, many new car manufacturers set up around Birmingham and Coventry because other car manufacturers were already there. Similarly, during the mid-1980s, many firms involved in information technology set up along the M4 corridor. Workers became very well-paid as a result of firms in the area trying to outbid each other to hire skilled workers.

Nowadays, one of the chief factors affecting the location of businesses is called **industrial inertia**. When a business was established, there may have been very good reasons for its location. These reasons may well no longer exist, and it may then be the case that there could be some advantages from moving. However, firms tend to avoid moving because it involves a lot of hassle. Having said that, during the 1970s and 1980s, Central London became so expensive that many businesses decided to keep a small office in the capital and move their operational headquarters to major towns out of London – e.g. Sun Life Assurance to Bristol and Royal London Insurance to Colchester.

It was in the late 1920s that the government first recognised the problem of regional imbalance in industrial structure and employment opportunities and began to enact measures designed to alleviate them. Unlike in many other European Countries, the root of Britain's regional problem was, and still is, the regional imbalance of declining traditional industries which prospered in the nineteenth century, rather than a decline in the agricultural industry.

(Briefing by the Department of Trade and Industry, 1990)

Government policy

Due to the factors outlined in this chapter, there have been gaps between economic activities in different regions of the UK – see Table 23.1.

Table 23.1 The percentage of the workforce classed by the government as unemployed in various regions of the UK, 1995

Region	Unemployment rate (%)
South-East	8.2
East Anglia	6.8
South-West	7.7
West Midlands	8.6
East Midlands	8.0
Yorkshire and Humberside	9.1
North-West	9.0
North	10.8
Wales	8.5
Scotland	8.4
Northern Ireland	11.8
UK average was	8.4

(CSO 1995)

Since the end of World War II, UK regional policy has largely been concerned with giving subsidies to businesses to set up in areas with above-average unemployment. The building of new factories has been encouraged by Selective Financial Assistance (SFA) which, unlike policy prior to 1984, is not automatic: businesses now have to present a case showing that the SFA will allow genuine new investment to take place rather than merely have the effect of diverting jobs from somewhere else. Areas in which these grants are available are called **assisted areas**.

Regional policy has three aims:

1. to divert industry (and jobs) from non-assisted to assisted areas;
2. to induce firms already located in assisted areas to expand;
3. to attract multinational businesses into the UK from other countries.

In recent years, there have been attempts to change the emphasis of British regional policy away from government incentives and over to market-based incentives. In other words, it is expected that businesses should naturally choose to move to areas where there is not much existing business. This is because, as there is a low demand for workers in these areas, wages will be low, and as there is also a low demand for land in these areas, property prices will be low. To encourage this trend, there has been a move towards ending nationally agreed pay scales in the public sector, as well as the introduction of local pay negotiations. In March 1995, there was great agitation in the National Health Service because nurses were given a national pay rise of just 1%, with a further 2% available if local hospital trusts agreed to pay it.

On the other hand, unemployed workers also would move to areas of low unemployment in search of work if they were desperate enough. Cutting unemployment benefit would encourage this, as would ending any controls on rent so that more rented accommodation could be offered in areas of low unemployment. Having said that, in 1995, despite this trend, even East Anglia, with the lowest unemployment in the country, still had an historically high rate of nearly 7%.

The European Union Regional Development Fund

Monika Wulf-Mathies, the second Bonn nominee, is the most high-powered woman in German public life. She has chaired the OTV public sector union, one of the largest in the world, for 12 years. She will be in charge of regional policy, a job currently held by Bruce Millan, a former Scottish Secretary and a British commissioner. This job carries a relatively low profile in Brussels, but is of greater importance in regions that receive large EU aid, such as Ireland, and parts of Scotland and eastern Germany.

(The Times, 1 November 1994)

The European Union (EU) is a major contributor to regional policy. In order to try to bring some of the poorest areas of the EU towards the prosperity of the richest, the EU pays for major construction projects. If you go to Northern Ireland, Scotland, the North of England, Wales or the South-West, you will see signs showing that roads and bridges have been financed by the EU. Other poorer areas of the EU are to be found in Spain, Portugal, Greece, Southern Italy and Eastern Germany. There is a 'Golden Triangle' of prosperity (see Figure 23.2) connecting the South-East of England with the Rhineland area of Germany and the North of

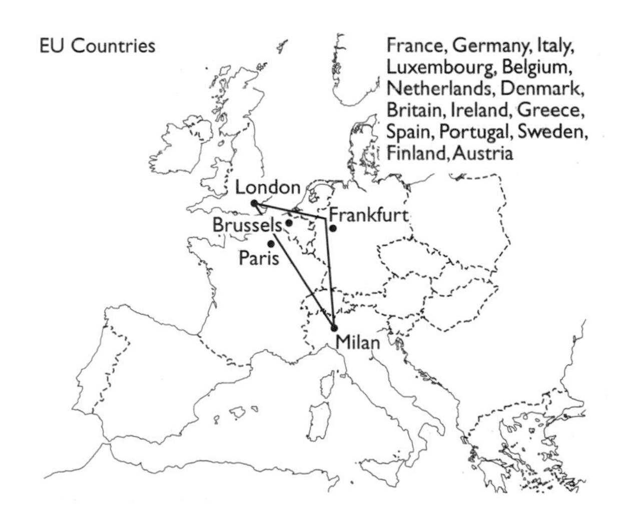

Figure 23.2 The EU 'Golden Triangle'

Italy. As a rough generalisation, the further you get from that triangle, the poorer you will find the region.

EC's £1.8bn to boost regions

The European Commission yesterday approved a £1.8 billion aid package for Northern Ireland, parts of Scotland and Merseyside in an attempt to improve the economic conditions there and bring them closer to European standards.

Northern Ireland will receive just under £1 billion, to be disbursed by 1999. The Highlands and Islands will receive £242 million and Merseyside £636 million.

The funds come from Europe's 'Objective 1' programme, which is aimed at reducing regional economic disparities. European aid to the regions is not new and yesterday's decision effectively amounts to a continuation of a programme that expired last year.

In the case of Merseyside, the Commission said the aim was to 'establish Merseyside as a prosperous European City Region'.

(The Times, 14 July 1994)

Summary

The pattern of location of industry in the UK has resulted in an uneven spread of economic activity around the country. For most of the twentieth century, governments have given incentives for businesses to set up or expand in assisted areas. If markets operated freely, perhaps more people would move to areas of lower unemployment where costs are lower.

The European Union plays an increasingly important role in promoting regional development.

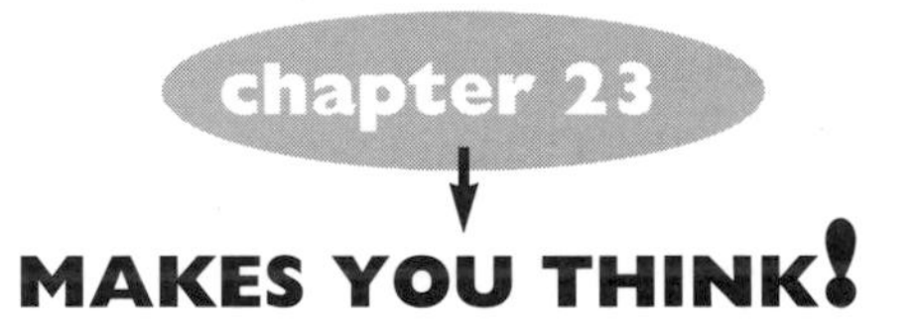

MAKES YOU THINK!

1 Which regions have unemployment rates

(a) above the national average
(b) below the national average?

2 Suggest reasons why Northern Ireland may have particularly high levels of unemployment.

3 What policies would you suggest that a government should adopt if it wished to reduce regional imbalances in prosperity?

Chapter 24

Economic growth

Table 24.1 Percentage annual changes in gross domestic product for the year ending June 1995

Australia	+3.7
UK	+2.8
Canada	+2.5
France	+3.0
Japan	+0.6
Sweden	+4.8
Switzerland	+1.4
USA	+3.2
China	+9.4
Hong Kong	+5.9
India	+5.0
Malaysia	+9.3
South Korea	+9.6
Poland	+5.0
Russia	−4.0

National income

When measuring **national income**, we are seeking to measure the amount of money flowing around the economy. To do this, there are three different approaches that we can take, involving measuring either income, output or expenditure.

Income

To measure all the income in the economy, payments for factors of production are recorded. As we saw, rent is paid for land, wages for labour, interest for capital and profit for enterprise. These payments are already known to the government because they are liable for tax, and it should be a relatively simple task to add them together. However, this measure is unreliable because some payments are never declared for tax. Think of every time you give somebody some cash for doing a little job. How much gets declared for income tax? And what about tasks where there is no financial reward? Suppose one person takes their car to a reputable garage for a minor repair, and is charged £50. It is likely that the job and the payment will be recorded in the national-income statistics. However, suppose a second person has exactly the same job done by a friend, and no cash changes hands. Here there is no income, but the job has still been done, but of course it is never recorded in the national-income statistics.

Output

The output method measures the value of the output of industry. There are two ways of measuring this: **final output** and **intermediate output**. Very simply, final output is the goods and services which are either purchased by consumers or used by industry as capital goods. It is in fact the final output only in which we are really interested because of the need to avoid **double counting**: when calculating national income, we must be careful to avoid counting the same things twice – i.e. at different stages in the production process. For example, a can of baked beans bought in a supermarket would be recorded as final output. The purchase of the beans and the can by the food manufacturer, on the other hand, are what would here be called the intermediate output. If the can of baked beans cost 50p in the supermarket, whilst the can itself cost the manufacturer 5p and the beans 10p, the total value of the output is still 50p and not 65p (50p + 10p + 5p). If we were to make it 65p, this would be an example of double counting because we would be counting the value of both the tin and the beans twice. An alternative way to avoid double counting is to measure the **value added** at each stage of production. So, 35p of value has been added to the can of beans between the manufacturer buying the beans and the can separately (for 10p + 5p) and the supermarket selling them to the customer (for 50p).

Expenditure

This approach is generally thought to be the most accurate of the three. All spending on consumption (spending by households on goods and services), investment (spending by firms on goods used in production), government spending and exports is added together. Spending on imports, which is difficult to measure, must then be taken away from the overall figure for expenditure.

Terms used in measuring national income

On the news, you will often hear the term 'gross domestic product' (GDP). This is a common measure of national performance, but it is not the only one. In fact, there are various measures that are used, and each is slightly different. We shall briefly consider each one, before summarising the information in a chart (see page 105).

Domestic and national income

A lot of production carried on in a particular country is carried out by foreign companies operating in that country, such as the Ford Motor Company (American-owned) or the Nissan car plant at Sunderland (Japanese-owned) in the UK. Whilst creating jobs and earning money for the local economies, these companies also generate profits which are sent back to the USA and Japan. Similarly, British companies have plants abroad (e.g. Hanson, a company from over here doing rather well over there). Profits from these companies in turn come back to the UK.

Domestic income differs from national income in that it does not include income paid and received from abroad. National income, on the other hand, does include both domestic income and income earned and paid abroad. This income earned and paid abroad is called **net property income from abroad**.

Market prices and factor cost

Market prices are what people actually pay for things. **Factor cost**, on the other hand, is the amount that goes towards paying the factors of production through wages, rent, interest and profit. In theory, those latter payments should equal the price of the product, but in reality that price will also be affected by the government. Some governments have tried to make some things cheaper than they otherwise would be by paying the producer a sum of money known as a subsidy. This practice has not been in favour since the 1970s, though the Common Agricultural Policy does, however, subsidise farmers, albeit in a very different way. The very common way in which governments affect the price of things is of course through indirect taxes such as VAT (value-added tax). There is a range of such taxes that can increase the price of goods.

Therefore, to go from market prices to factor cost, you take off (subtract) taxes and you add to the price any subsidies. To go from factor cost to market prices, you do the opposite: add taxes and subtract subsidies.

Gross and net

Sometimes you will see figures for **gross national income**, and sometimes you will see them for **net national income**. The difference between the two is **depreciation**, which is sometimes also called **capital consumption**. This is the allowance that is made for the fact that the capital stock (i.e. the country's stock of factories, machines etc.) wears out. This factor affects investment, as a lot of investment involves money that is spent on simply replacing worn-out equipment. Economists, however, are more interested in **net investment**, i.e. the amount of *new* capital stock that is created. Therefore, net national income excludes depreciation.

Transfer payments

There are some incomes that people receive that are transferred by the government from what *other* people have earned. These must not be included in the national-income accounts because they will already have been counted once. Such **transfer payments** comprise payments such as pensions and unemployment and other social-security benefits.

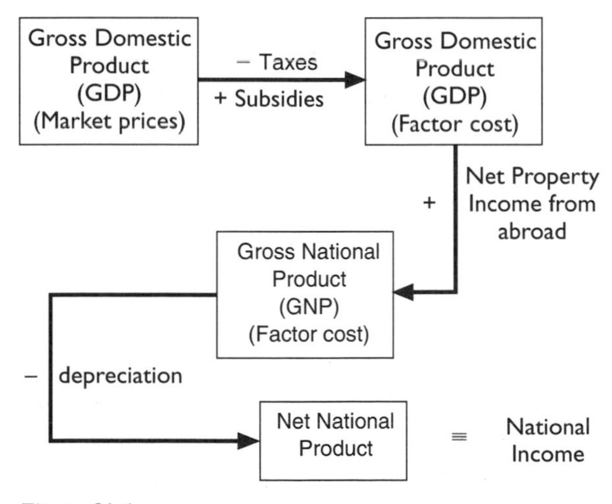

Figure 24.1

Why measure national income?

Table 24.2 Percentage growth rates in gross domestic product at market prices, 1960–93

	Europe 12	UK	USA	Japan
1960	–	–	–	–
1961	5.5	3.3	2.8	12.0
1962	4.7	1.0	5.3	8.9
1963	4.5	3.9	4.3	8.5
1964	5.8	5.5	5.8	11.7
1965	4.4	2.5	6.0	5.8
1966	4.0	1.9	5.1	10.6
1967	3.3	2.3	2.3	11.1
1968	5.3	4.1	4.2	12.9
1969	6.3	2.1	2.9	12.5
1970	7.2	2.3	−0.1	10.7
1971	3.2	2.0	3.3	4.3
1972	4.3	3.5	5.1	8.4
1973	6.2	7.3	4.8	7.9
1974	1.9	−1.7	−0.7	−1.2
1975	−1.0	−0.8	−1.0	2.6
1976	4.9	2.7	4.9	4.8
1977	2.8	2.3	4.4	5.3
1978	3.2	3.6	5.1	5.1
1979	3.5	2.9	2.0	5.2
1980	1.3	−2.2	−0.1	4.4
1981	0.1	−1.3	2.3	3.9
1982	0.7	1.7	−2.6	2.8
1983	1.6	3.7	3.9	3.2
1984	2.3	2.2	7.2	5.0
1985	2.4	3.6	3.8	15.4
1986	2.8	3.9	3.2	2.6
1987	2.9	4.8	3.5	4.1
1988	4.0	4.2	4.5	6.2
1989	3.3	2.3	2.8	4.6
1990	2.8	0.8	0.9	5.6
1991	1.3	−1.8	−0.4	4.6
1992	2.2	2.0	2.1	3.5
1993	2.4	2.8	2.2	3.5

(EuroStat)

There are two reasons for measuring national income: to compare how the country is doing over time, and to compare how the country is doing against other countries (see Table 24.2). Comparing how a country is doing over time is relatively easy as you are comparing like with like. You will often hear on the news that the economy is growing at a certain percentage rate.

For example, if the economy is growing at a rate of 3%, that means that the national income is 3% higher than it was a year ago. If the national income is below what it was a year ago, then we have a negative economic growth. For example, if the national income is 1% below what it was last year, we have an economic growth of −1%. This measurement is made quarterly, i.e. every 3 months. Two quarters (i.e. 6 months) of negative economic growth is the definition of a recession.

We would, however, expect the national income to go up each year because *prices* tend to go up each year. Therefore, before we can make any meaningful comment about whether there has been economic growth, we need to know how much of any change is **real** as opposed to **nominal**. A real increase is an increase above the rate of inflation (i.e. above the average level of price increases). So, if national income rose by 5% but prices rose by 7% (i.e. the rate of inflation was 7%), then real economic growth would be −2%.

Comparing national income between countries is more problematic. First, countries have different populations. You would expect a country with a population five times as large as the UK's (e.g. the USA) to have a higher national income, and so a more useful comparison is national income **per head** or **per capita**, which is simply national income divided by the population total. Second, countries use different currencies, and so the exchange rate, which changes from day to day, can also make a comparison difficult. Then, some countries have to spend more on some goods or services without really making anyone better off. For example, Sweden spends a lot more on heating than does Spain. However, perhaps the most significant problem is that only output that is *recorded* can be included in national income. In this country, this means that DIY jobs go unrecorded, but so too does the **black economy**. This is the name given to activities (as mentioned earlier) that are not declared for tax. In many countries, a lot of activity is carried on within the village or the family where money may not be exchanged at all, and where paperwork is certainly not a priority. It is therefore impossible to do any more than *estimate* the national income for many countries.

Economic growth

Increased output, and therefore **economic growth**, comes about as a result of an increase in either the quantity or the quality of the factors of production. Land is often a limited resource, and it is therefore unusual to be able to increase the quantity of land, although the Netherlands has drained the sea for many centuries to almost double its size. However, land can be made more productive by changing its use. In Saudi Arabia, experiments are taking place to change the desert into fertile agricultural land; and in this country, derelict land can have productive industrial estates built on it.

Increasing the size of the workforce is a long-term process, but from time to time governments will encourage families to increase the population and, after sixteen years of bringing up the son or daughter, the workforce. Under President Ceauşescu in Rumania, birth control was illegal and women were told that it was their duty to have many children. The same was true in Nazi Germany where it was the duty of Aryan women to breed. In the UK, child benefit was introduced to make it easier for families to afford to bring up children because a potential 'demographic time bomb' has been identified. At a time of high unemployment, it is difficult to remember that the proportion of pensioners to 16–65-year-olds is increasing.

Over the last 30 years in the UK, there has

been a large increase in the workforce as many married women now work. During the 1950s and 1960s, there was a shortage of labour, and so people were actively recruited, by organisations such as London Transport and the National Health Service, from the Indian subcontinent and the West Indies; so immigration is another way of increasing the quantity of labour.

However, despite these trends, it is more common in the UK to concentrate on increasing the *quality* of labour through training and education.

Increases in investment are likely to come about in response to lower rates of interest. Some economists (**neo-classical**) argue that investment levels go up when interest rates go down, and that investment falls when interest rates go up. This is because when interest rates are high, repayments on any loans will be expensive, whereas if money is left in a bank, it will earn a good return. Thus, if interest rates are high, a project would have to seem very profitable to make it worthwhile – or to put it another way, money invested has to work harder when interest rates are high. This is called the **marginal efficiency of capital**.

Keynesian economists tend to see demand as the key to everything, and so they argue that investment goes up when demand in the economy goes up, and falls when demand falls. These economists have developed the **accelerator principle** which says that in order to meet increased demand for a firm's output, some extra investment will be needed. For example, a ferry company may find that as people become better off, so more people decide to take their cars to the Continent. The demand in a year may thus increase by £1 million, and to meet this extra demand, a new ship is bought costing £10 million. However, the ferry company hopes that the extra demand will last for *more* than 10 years so that over a long period of time a profit will be made. An increase in demand of £1 million has resulted in an extra investment of £10 million, and this is the accelerator effect.

As consumption and investment both tend to increase when interest rates are low, both the neo-classical economists and the Keynesians can claim to be right here – as usual. However, it really doesn't matter which side is right because economists are *generally* agreed that the way to increase investment is to lower interest rates.

In the early 1980s, Mrs Thatcher's Conservative government claimed to promote enterprise or encourage entrepreneurs by policies such as reducing taxes on high levels of income and providing advice for setting up new businesses.

The production possibility frontier

The production possibility frontier (or curve) shows the maximum output of an economy. From any point inside the frontier, production can be increased by using some unused resources. It is not possible to move beyond the frontier without discovering some new resources. On the frontier it is only possible to

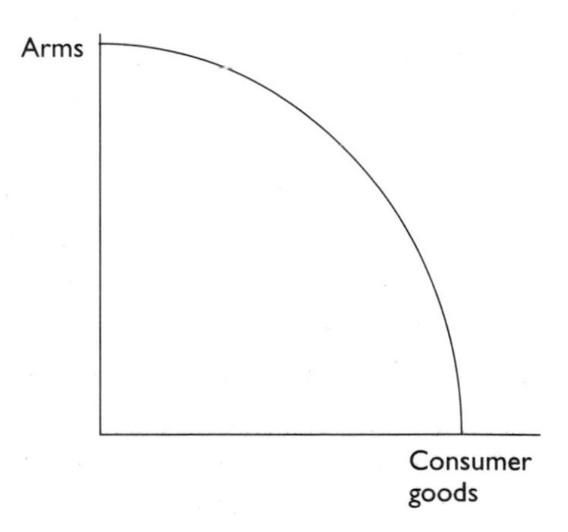

Figure 24.2 A production possibility frontier showing the trade-off between military and consumer goods

increase the production of one thing by reducing the production of something else. If the quantity or the quality of the factors of production can be increased then it is possible to move to a new frontier which is further out from the origin.

Another point is demonstrated by the frontier, and that is that 'trade-offs' take place. A country that devotes a lot of its resources to weapons will obviously have less resources available for consumer goods.

National income and the standard of living

Although there are difficulties (as discussed above) in measuring national income, it *is* possible. The **standard of living** is a much broader view of how well-off is the average citizen. This includes things such as health provision, education availability and numbers of TV sets and cars. Whilst, however, there is a general agreement that it is a good thing that only 0.9% of children in the UK now die before reaching the age of 1 – as opposed to 14.2% in 1900 – the question of whether a continual increase in car ownership is a good thing is more problematic.

Problems of economic growth

There can be little doubt that developing countries such as Ethiopia or Bangladesh are in desperate need of economic growth. In Western countries, such growth is generally seen as desirable, and governments certainly have it as one of their main aims. However, there are many who would argue that growth at all costs is not desirable, and another group (which includes the Green Party) would argue that economic growth is leading to environmental disaster. As economic growth comes about by using up resources, it is clear that one day these resources will run out. Furthermore, it is increasingly being realised that what is being put into the world through growth is a bigger problem than what is being used up. Increased production leads to increasing levels of carbon dioxide which – as we have seen in Chapter 18 – are causing global warming, and scientists fear that this will lead to rising sea levels and larger deserts. What's more, increases in incomes in countries such as India are leading to increasing purchases of consumer products, and the technology of refrigeration is thus becoming widely available. Unfortunately, the cheapest fridges purchased contain CFCs which lead to the destruction of the ozone layer, which in turn leads to an increased risk of skin cancer. However, is it fair or reasonable to expect poorer countries to go without the technology so long enjoyed in the West?

Summary

Economic growth is an increase in a country's national income. National income is a measurement of either a country's output, its expenditure or its income; all of which, in theory, should come to the same total. Economic growth can be brought about by increasing either the quantity or the quality of the factors of production.

In the West, a debate has begun concerning the desirability of continued economic growth.

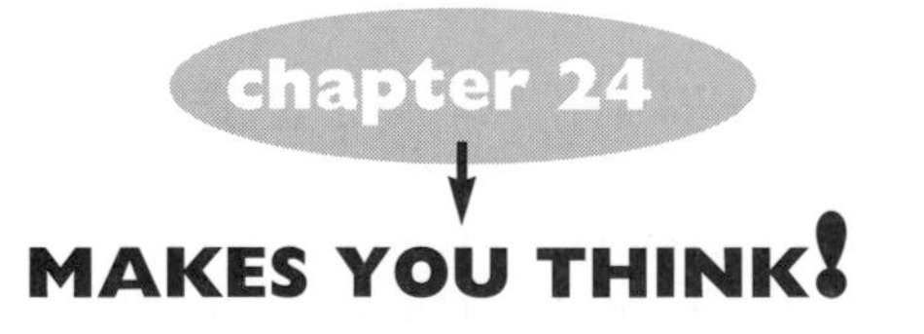

1. Why do some people argue that economic growth is in fact bad?
2. Explain why national income is different from the standard of living.

3 The Lucas family comprises George, a hospital manager aged 45; Danielle, a teacher and mother aged 48; Doris, retired, aged 75; Gary, unemployed, aged 20; Francesca, a university student, aged 18; Duncan, a sixth former, aged 17. List all the sources of income for the Lucas family under two headings:
(a) part of national income
(b) transfer payments

Chapter 25

The balance of payments

The subject of **balance of payments** is often featured on the news. You should watch out for up-to-date accounts of the balance-of-payments position, and listen to the commentators as they try to explain the current balance-of-payments situation.

Table 25.1 The balance of invisible trade, in ECU millions, for Europe (12), the UK and Japan, 1980–90

	Europe 12	UK	Japan
1980	–	2,685	−9,276
1981	3,778	5,093	−13,642
1982	−1,301	3,080	−11,467
1983	8,934	8,326	−11,965
1984	16,404	11,539	−11,741
1985	17,666	10,820	−8,999
1986	11,207	14,523	−7,083
1987	6,791	10,511	−8,156
1988	−845	9,210	−13,115
1989	2,322	6,360	−18,095
1990	–	4,933	−21,354

(EuroStat)

Table 25.1 shows how the UK's **invisible trade balance** (i.e. involving services rather than goods) has remained fairly healthy during the 1980s, whilst visible trade has moved from surplus to a very bad deficit. Historically, for many years, the UK has imported more goods than it has exported. However, this has tended to be made up for by successfully exporting invisible services such as banking, insurance and tourism. During the early 1980s, the government used high interest rates to reduce demand and force down inflation. The effect of these high interest rates was to force up the exchange rate and reduce exports, whilst also attracting in imports.

Usually during a recession, demand for imports will fall along with demand generally. However, there is no need for exports to fall as foreign markets are not necessarily affected by domestic economic conditions, so the current account (see below) improves. The recession of the early 1990s, however, saw only a little improvement in the UK's current-account position.

Excluding erratic items such as the jump in exports of precious stones and the fall in aircraft imports, the trade deficit fell slightly from £1.53 billion in March to £1.46 billion in April. However, latest official estimates show the visible trade deficit is now narrowing at a rate of 1% a month.

(Adapted from The Guardian, 9 July 1994)

The meaning of the balance of payments

The balance of payments is simply a record of payments of money made by one country to virtually all the other countries in the world. Countries need to pay for all the products that they do not produce themselves. They also borrow and lend money abroad, or buy property or businesses in other countries. All these activities bring about flows of money between countries, and these are recorded in the balance-of-payments account. These flows of money are divided into two accounts. The record of payments for goods and services is called the

current account. On the other hand, any money which moves in or out of the country for other reasons is recorded on the **capital account**.

The current account

This account is itself divided into two parts. **Visible trade** is trade in goods (raw materials, food, manufactured goods etc.), i.e. things that you can physically see leaving or arriving in the country. **Invisible trade** is the export and import of services (tourism, banking etc.), i.e. those things that you cannot see leaving or arriving in the country but for which payment is nonetheless made.

Table 25.2 The UK, USA and Japan current accounts in ECU millions, 1980–90

	UK	USA	Japan
1980	5,178	1,432	−7,663
1981	11,268	5,439	4,813
1982	7,227	−9,828	7,228
1983	6,519	−53,777	23,792
1984	3,303	−126,422	44,927
1985	5,500	−159,682	63,667
1986	233	−147,836	86,616
1987	−5,977	−138,960	75,462
1988	−23,402	−107,453	66,624
1989	−30,459	−96,640	52,216
1990	−21,093	−72,514	28,430

(EuroStat)

The definitions are as follows:

visible exports minus visible imports = the **balance of trade**

invisible exports minus visible imports = the **invisible balance** (or **invisible earnings**)

total exports minus total imports = the **current balance**

According to the Central Statistical Office (CSO), there was a deficit on current account of £4.1 billion, up from £3.9 billion in the final quarter of 1993 and the highest quarterly shortfall since the second quarter of 1990, when it reached £5.5 billion. The deficit on visible trade was £4.5 billion, compared with £4.4 billion in the last quarter of 1992.

Invisible earnings were published showing a recovery in Britain's surplus on services to £1.2 billion from £600 million in the final quarter of last year, largely due to insurance earnings.

The capital account

This is a record of savings and investment made either abroad or by foreigners in this country. Although most individuals would not think of comparing interest rates around the world to find the best return on their money, large financial institutions (such as insurance companies), managers of pension funds and even very wealthy individuals find that it is very worthwhile to do so – 1% of $1 billion is a lot of money! When a country raises its rate of interest, money from abroad is likely to be attracted in, and this is called **hot money**.

Examples of investments carried out abroad are all around us, such as the American Ford Motor Company owning factories in the UK, Germany and many other countries, the Japanese Sony factory in South Wales, the American Disney organisation owning Disneyland Paris in France, and of course McDonald's which is everywhere.

On the UK capital account, savings and

investment are recorded as **investment and other capital transactions**, and this forms the main part of the capital account.

The official reserves

The balance of payments must be in balance, i.e. money flowing into the country must equal money flowing out. Obviously, at any one time this may not be the case; and if, for example, more money is flowing out than in, then this money has to come from somewhere. Take the example of someone in the UK buying a Renault car made in France. The customer will go to her local Renault dealer and pay for the car in pounds. However, the people who make the car in France will want to be paid in French francs because they cannot spend pounds in France. At some point, therefore, Renault UK will have to acquire French francs to pay for the imported cars. These francs are available to UK businesses, from banks and foreign currency dealers, because French companies in turn are buying British goods for which they need pounds. Therefore, in order for Britons to be able to buy all the imports they desire, sufficient foreign currency must be made available by foreigners who are either buying British exports or saving money in the UK.

At times when there is less money flowing into the country than is flowing out, the **official reserves** of currencies will reduce. These reserves can be built up when the money flowing in *exceeds* the money flowing out. Obviously, reserves cannot be allowed to fall indefinitely, because eventually they would run out. Countries with large foreign-currency reserves can face flows of billions of dollars in a day.

Balance-of-payments problems

It should now be clear that if a country is running a deficit on its current account, it will have to pay for it by running a surplus on the capital account. The easiest way to attract money to flow in on the capital account is to raise interest rates, but this may run counter to the government's other economic policy aims. On the other hand, it may be possible to improve the current-account balance by allowing the value of the currency to fall. This is dealt with in Chapter 27 on exchange rates.

A large surplus on the current account can itself have consequences, although not particularly bad ones. Japan has run a huge current-account surplus for many years (see Table 25.2). This means that it must run a large deficit on its capital account, and to achieve this its interest rates have tended to be very low. However, Japan still has large reserves of foreign money which would just go on building up if it were not for the fact that Japanese companies have used this money to buy large areas of American land and businesses particularly in Hawaii, Hollywood and New York.

Table 25.3 Japanese current and capital accounts in ECU millions, 1980–90

	Japan	
	Current	**Capital**
1980	−7,663	1,658
1981	4,813	−6,167
1982	7,228	−16,349
1983	23,792	−21,342
1984	44,927	−64,277
1985	63,667	−82,462
1986	86,616	−132,840
1987	75,462	−115,760
1988	66,624	−99,760
1989	52,216	−85,341
1990	28,430	−42,995

(EuroStat)

Summary

The balance of payments is a record of all financial transactions between economic agents in one country and those in all other countries. The balance of payments comprises the current account and the capital account. These two accounts must add up to zero (i.e. neither a surplus nor a deficit), and adjustments to the official reserves (part of the capital account) will automatically ensure this. Current-account deficits can cause problems for a government in trying to achieve other economic goals.

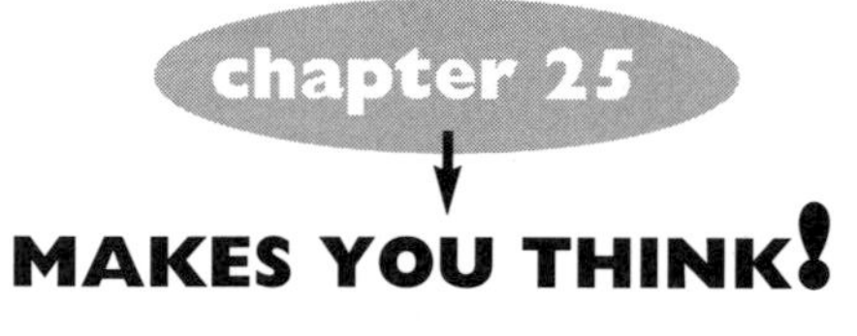

1 Which of the following are (i) visible exports, (ii) visible imports, (iii) invisible exports and (iv) invisible imports?

(a) a crate of bananas from the Caribbean
(b) a British tourist holidaying in Greece
(c) BMWs being sold in the UK
(d) a British insurance firm selling a policy to an American

2 Suppose that:
- visible exports = £800 billion
- visible imports = £900 billion
- invisible exports = £400 billion
- invisible imports = £200 billion

(a) What is the balance of trade?
(b) What is the current account balance?

3 Look at Table 25.2.

(a) Which country had the largest current-account surplus in 1986?
(b) In which year did the UK move into deficit on current account?

What would you expect to see happen to the German and Japanese capital accounts after 1993? What would you expect to happen to German and Japanese investment overseas?

Chapter 26

International trade

In 1947, 23 countries signed the **General Agreement on Tariffs and Trade** (GATT). This was in response to the view that previous wars had often been caused by countries failing to trade with one another. The GATT rules prevented member countries from increasing restrictions on trade with one another, and since 1947 new GATT agreements have sought to reduce trade restrictions between countries and thus to encourage world trade. Some areas of the world have sought to greatly reduce trade barriers to a point where they do not exist (see Chapter 28), but this has only applied to member countries: restrictions on imports from outside a particular group of countries have still been strictly enforced.

Comparative advantage

Adam Smith is often thought of as the father of modern economics. In his book *The Wealth of Nations*, a famous example is given. It is shown how in a pin factory, the processes involved in producing a pin are split up so that different workers specialise in different tasks. This principle of the division of labour, i.e. the principle that output can be increased through specialisation (see Chapter 3), can also be applied to whole countries. A technical explanation (which you may ignore if you wish) is as follows.

Suppose that just two countries, the UK and France, decide to trade with each other, and that they only trade in two goods: bread and sausages. As shown in the table, France has an **absolute advantage** in the production of bread, because it takes only 2 man hours to make a unit of bread in France, whereas in the UK it takes 3. On the other hand, the UK has an absolute advantage in the production of sausages. If the UK were to import all its bread from France and divert the resources that it once used to make bread to making sausages instead, and if France in turn gave up making sausages and concentrated on making bread, both countries would be better off.

Number of man hours required to produce 1 unit of:

	Bread	Sausages
UK	3	2
France	2	4

Even in a situation where one country has an absolute advantage in the production of both goods, it may still be advantageous to both countries to specialise. Let's assume that Swedway is more efficient than Norden in the production of both goods used above – i.e. it has an absolute advantage in bread and sausages. The above principle of specialisation still applies as long as the opportunity costs involved differ. Suppose, for example, that with a given fixed amount of resources:

- Norden can produce either 20 sausages *or* 200 loaves of bread; whilst
- Swedway can produce either 10 sausages or 150 loaves of bread

In terms of resources used, the costs of production for *both* products is lower in Norden. If we look at the opportunity cost, however, a different picture emerges. In Norden, the cost of 1 sausage is 10 loaves of bread, while in Swedway the cost of 1 sausage is 15 loaves of bread. In terms of the sausages given up to make bread, bread is therefore cheaper in Swedway. Swedway thus has a **comparative advantage** in bread.

The terms of trade

The **terms of trade** involve the use of index numbers which were introduced in Chapter 21 on inflation. The terms of trade record the direction in which a country's trade position moves over time. First, a base year is chosen, say 1990. Then the prices of exports in 1990 are added together, and whatever that figure is, say £100 billion, it is called 100. Similarly, the import prices for 1990 are added together. Let's assume that exports and imports were in balance in 1990, so that import prices add up to £100 billion also; again, the import price index for 1990 will be 100 whatever the actual total is. Now let's assume that in 1991, export prices had risen to £110 billion. The index of export prices will now be 110. If import prices have increased to £105 billion, then the index for import prices will be 105. The terms of trade are now worked out by the formula:

$$\frac{\textbf{index of export prices}}{\textbf{index of import prices}} \times \mathbf{100} = \textbf{terms of trade}$$

If we now apply this formula, we find that in the base year, 100 divided by 100 equals 1, and that 1 multiplied by 100 equals 100. However, in 1991, we find that:

$$\frac{\mathbf{110}}{\mathbf{105}} \times \mathbf{100} = \mathbf{104.7619}$$

Thus, the terms of trade have improved from 100 to 104. In 1992, the index of export prices has increased to 115, while the index of import prices has increased to 120. Hence:

$$\frac{\mathbf{115}}{\mathbf{120}} \times \mathbf{100} = \mathbf{95.83r}$$

so that the terms of trade have now worsened.

The terms of trade illustrate a major problem for developing countries. This is that over the last quarter of a century, price rises in the West have been running at very high levels. As a result, because they are buying large quantities of goods from Western countries, developing countries have seen their index of import prices rising quickly each year. On the other hand, the few goods they can export (e.g. coffee, tea) have seen their prices fall in recent years, and so the index of export prices has worsened. As their terms of trade have thus worsened, these countries have had to export more in order to buy the same amount of imports. In order to achieve this, the developing countries have devoted increasing resources to growing cash crops (e.g. coffee, tea) at the expense of growing food for domestic consumption.

Restricting international trade

Having looked at the advantages of international trade, we now need to consider the fact that various restrictions on trade exist. These restrictions can take the following forms:

Quotas

A quota (see also Chapter 19) is a limit placed on the quantity of a good that can be imported.

Voluntary export restraint

This is a fairly new development whereby a country voluntarily agrees to limit its exports of a product. For example, the UK has an agreement with Japanese car producers that the Japanese will not take more than 10% of the UK market for cars. This is a voluntary quota adopted by the exporting country to avoid something worse being imposed by the importing country.

Both quotas and voluntary export restraints lead both to consumers having their choice limited and to the payment of higher prices – see Figure 26.1.

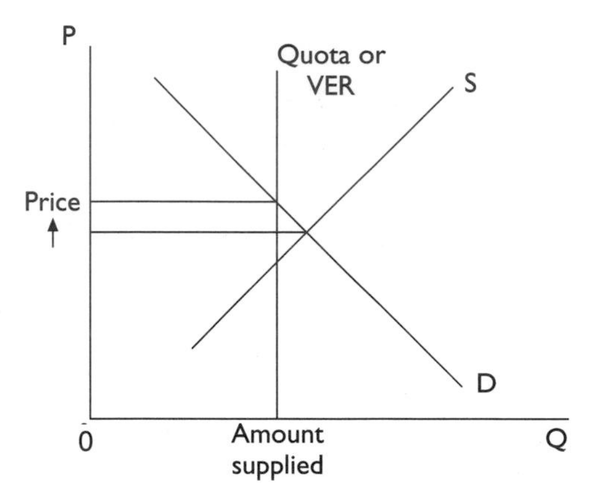

Figure 26.1 How a quota or voluntary export restraint leads to restricted supply and a higher price

Tariffs

A **tariff** is a tax on imported goods; it is sometimes also called an **import duty** or a **customs duty**. Tariffs are used to discourage consumers from buying imported products by raising their price – see Figure 26.2. The effect is slightly different from a quota since, with a quota, the higher price benefits the producer whereas with a tariff, it is the government that gains from the higher price.

Other methods of restricting trade

Rather than adopt policies to make imported goods more expensive, a government could instead decide to make goods produced within

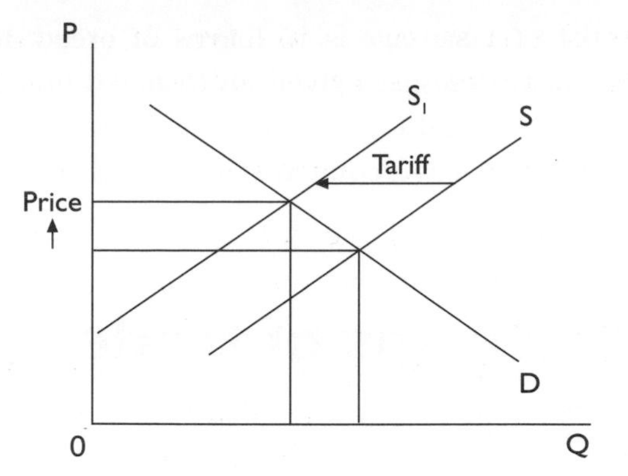

Figure 26.2 How a tariff reduces supply and raises the price

the country cheaper by granting a subsidy. For example, in the mid-1990s, fares on Air France were cheaper than they otherwise might have been because the French government paid the debts of the business.

Another way of restricting imports is by adopting **non-tariff barriers**. These can be anything designed to make it more difficult for consumers to buy imported goods. For example, during the 1980s, the French government decided that all Japanese video machines had to be imported through a small airport hundreds of miles from Paris.

Reasons for trade restrictions

Policies to restrict free trade are called **protectionist** as they are designed to protect a country's industry from foreign competition. There are a number of reasons for protection:

To raise revenue

In the UK, HM Customs and Excise has been taxing imported goods for more than 300 years. (The smuggling in of products, such as tobacco and alcohol, which can be obtained more cheaply abroad has a long history.) However, import duties are quite insignificant in terms of overall taxation, and in fact the money raised goes to the European Union's budget.

The infant industry argument

One argument for protection in certain circumstances is that industries just starting up will not benefit from the economies of scale enjoyed by similar already-existing industries in other countries. Therefore, it is argued that to allow a new industry to develop properly in a country, it is justifiable to protect that industry from foreign competition while it is starting up. The problem here, however, is that one day, competition from the real world will come as something of a shock.

The prevention of dumping

Dumping involves selling a product for less than the cost of producing it. The British motorcycle industry was largely destroyed by Japanese firms exporting motorbikes to the UK and selling them for less than they cost to produce. This forced British manufacturers out of business, leaving the market open to the Japanese who could then increase prices.

UK trade with Japan moves into surplus

Britain has achieved a turnaround in trade with Japan, chalking up a $310 million current account surplus in the first half of this year, compared with a $2.4 billion deficit at the same stage last year.

Official monthly figures issued in Tokyo yesterday showed that Japan's politically-sensitive current account rose an overall 15.4 per cent year-on-year in November to $9.7 billion.

(The Times, 29 December 1994)

Summary

The theory of comparative advantage suggests that countries will benefit from specialising in the production of what they are best at. Countries seek to limit free trade through protectionist measures such as the use of tariffs, quotas or non-tariff barriers.

The General Agreement on Tariffs and Trade (GATT) seeks to reduce barriers to international trade.

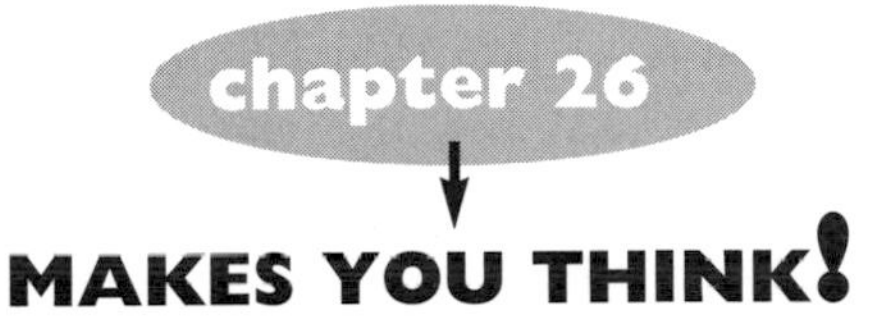

1. Why do manufactured goods usually have much higher tariffs charged on their importation than do raw materials?
2. Does protectionism help to reduce unemployment?
3. Does protectionism assist consumers?

Chapter 27

Exchange rates

From 1972 until 1990, the UK had a **floating exchange rate** which was managed from day to day by the Bank of England. In 1979, the EC member countries established the **European Monetary System** (EMS) and its **Exchange Rate Mechanism** (ERM). The UK did not join the ERM until 1990, and then at a high exchange rate. However, it pulled out in September 1992 because of speculation by foreign-currency dealers. When the pound then began floating again, it depreciated sharply, and this made it easier for UK firms to export. All of this will be explained in this chapter.

Table 27.1 Effective exchange rates, weighted according to export volumes, for 1972–91 (1980 = 100)

	Europe 12	FRG	UK	USA	Japan
1972	100.3	66.4	131.8	116.7	82.8
1973	103.0	73.4	118.0	107.4	87.4
1974	101.1	77.4	113.9	109.6	81.6
1975	102.5	78.6	104.8	108.7	79.3
1976	92.8	83.1	89.7	114.4	83.3
1977	91.9	89.7	85.5	113.6	92.4
1978	92.4	95.0	85.7	103.1	112.5
1979	98.4	99.6	90.9	100.2	104.2
1980	100.0	100.0	100.0	100.0	100.0
1981	83.9	94.4	100.2	112.8	113.6
1982	78.0	99.1	95.8	126.3	107.9
1983	71.4	103.1	89.1	133.6	119.7
1984	64.8	101.4	84.9	144.0	126.6
1985	63.5	101.7	84.8	149.9	130.5
1986	69.7	112.6	78.6	121.3	166.0
1987	74.5	120.4	77.8	106.7	179.7
1988	73.3	119.5	82.3	100.2	198.4
1989	71.1	118.0	79.5	105.1	189.7
1990	79.3	124.7	78.8	98.6	170.3
1991	76.2	122.9	79.0	98.3	185.4

FRG = Federal Republic of Germany
(EuroStat)

The meaning of exchange rates

Table 27.2 Exchange rates for £1 sterling as supplied by National Westminster Bank on 5 April 1995

Australia	2.12	Israel	4.75
Austria	15.10	Italy	2,700.00
Belgium	44.00	Malta	0.5475
Canada	2.18	Netherlands	2.42
Cyprus	0.70	New Zealand	2.40
Denmark	8.54	Norway	9.7
France	7.5	Portugal	228.00
Germany	2.16	Spain	197.25
Greece	357.00	Sweden	11.63
Hong Kong	12.20	Switzerland	1.765
India	50.38	Turkey	64,774.00
Ireland	0.975	USA	1.57

An **exchange rate** is simply the price of one currency expressed in terms of another currency (see Table 27.2). For example, if you are going on holiday to France, you will need to buy French francs to spend while you are in that country. These you will purchase either at a bank before you go, or on the boat during the crossing, or in a bank in France. Whichever way you do it, you will have to pay for the francs in pounds, and so you will need to know how many francs you can buy for your British money. In January 1994, you could buy 8.62 French francs for £1, so that was the exchange rate (£1 = FF8.62) at the time. If the exchange rate increases (or **appreciates**), you will get more francs for the pound, and so they become cheaper. If the exchange rate falls (or **depreciates**), you will get fewer francs, and so they become more expensive.

From your personal point of view, when planning a trip abroad, if the pound appreciates it is good news; but if it depreciates, it is bad news because you will get less foreign currency in exchange for your pounds. However, for the economy as a whole, the advantages and disadvantages of rising and falling exchange rates are far less clear-cut.

How are exchange rates determined?

The exchange rate is the price of a currency, and like all prices it is fixed by supply and demand (see again Figure 6.1). When the demand for the pound is high, it will cost a lot of Deutsche Marks or US dollars to buy. When demand for the pound is low, it will cost fewer Deutsche Marks or US dollars. Therefore, we must ask the question: what causes the demand for pounds to change?

There are three main factors that determine the level of exchange rates:

1 If people in Germany wish to buy British goods, they will need British money to buy those goods. This is true whether they come here on holiday or whether they are buying those goods in Germany. Whilst it is true that Germans can go to their local *Horten* or *Kaufhof* and pay for British-produced goods with their Deutsche Marks, the company that originally bought those goods from a British supplier would have had to pay that manufacturer in pounds. Therefore, at the most fundamental level, it is the demand for a country's exports of goods and services that determines the demand for that country's currency, and therefore also the exchange rate.

2 In the short run, a high interest rate will encourage big financial institutions to save their money in your country where it will earn a high return. If foreigners wish to hold money in UK bank accounts, they must first convert their money into pounds. Therefore, if the government raises interest rates, more people will demand pounds in order to hold savings in UK bank accounts. And as the

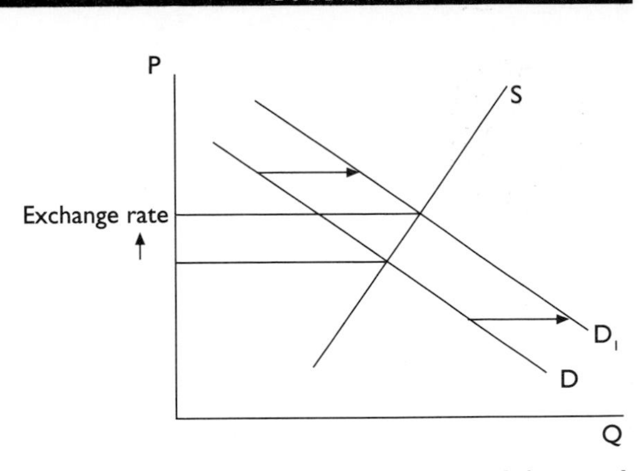

Figure 27.1 How an increase in the demand for pounds leads to a rise in the exchange rate for pounds

demand for pounds rises, so will the exchange rate – see Figure 27.1.

A major problem with using interest rates to keep the exchange rate high is that a high interest rate reduces demand in the economy, and this leads to unemployment and low economic growth.

In the long run, if the exchange rate is high because interest rates are high, then the financial institutions will become worried. They will know that a government will be tempted to cut interest rates if demand in the economy is low. However, once interest rates are reduced, there will be less demand for pounds. The exchange rate will fall, and each pound will buy fewer Deutsche Marks or US dollars. As a result the savings held by foreigners in UK bank accounts will not be worth as much. The sensible course of action will be to move the savings out before the pound reduces in value, but this action will lead to an increase in the supply of pounds and to a fall in the exchange rate – see Figure 27.2. This is why a country's export position is more fundamental in determining the exchange rates than are interest rates in the long run.

3 Speculators or foreign-currency dealers can also help to influence the exchange rate in the short run.

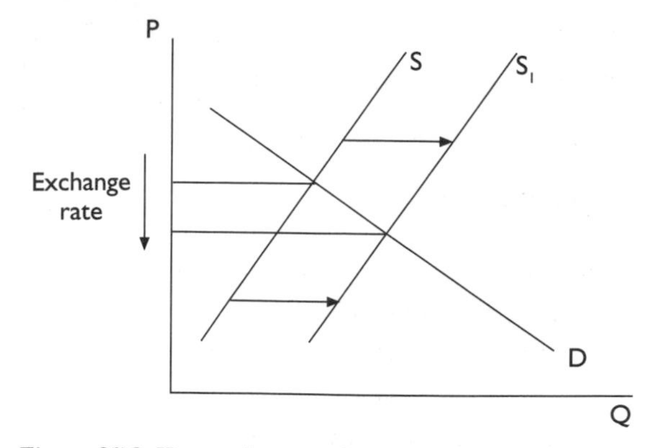

Figure 27.2 How an increase in the supply of pounds leads to a fall in the exchange rate for pounds

If you are a foreign-currency dealer and you think that the value of the pound is likely to fall, what is your best course of action? You would exchange your pounds for some other currency before the pound falls in value. Other dealers will have the same information as you, and being sensible people, they will sell their pounds also. There is now an increased supply of pounds, and so the exchange rate falls, proving to everyone that you took the correct course of action in selling your pounds. Now suppose that you thought that the price of pounds would *rise*. What would here be the sensible course of action for the foreign-currency dealer? Foreign currency dealers will now buy pounds while they are cheap and wait for the exchange rate to increase so that the pounds they now own will be worth more. Of course, this increased demand for pounds will *cause* the exchange rate to increase, so once again the dealers have taken the best action.

In the short term, currency dealers can determine the price of a currency by their buying and selling decisions, but if firms need more pounds to buy more British products, then they will demand them and so increase the exchange rate. So again we are back to the fact that it is a country's international trade position that determines the value of the currency in the long term.

Given that we have here discussed the expectations of foreign-currency dealers, what is it that leads them to believe that demand for a currency is likely to rise or fall? It is their expectations of what will happen to interest rates and exports.

The effects of exchange-rate changes

When the value of a currency falls or **devalues**, this means that you can exchange it for less of another country's currency. Thus, in August 1992, £1 could be exchanged for around 2.8 Deutsche Marks, whilst in August 1993, £1 would only buy about 2.3 Deutsche Marks. What difference does this make?

The most obvious difference to individuals in the UK was for anyone going on holiday to Germany. A hotel room costing 100 Deutsche Marks a night would have cost £35.71 in August 1992, but by August 1993, the same room at the same price in Deutsche Marks would have cost £43.48 in pounds sterling. On its part, a company that is importing or exporting may be dealing in thousands or millions of pounds, and if the pound falls in value by 10%, then, if the company is faced with a bill for imports of £1,000,000, an extra £100,000 will now be added to that bill.

Thus, if the pound depreciates, imports become more expensive. This will increase prices in the economy and so increase inflation. Exports then become cheaper in foreign markets, and so more will be bought, resulting in extra demand for UK products and possibly a fall in unemployment. A rise in the exchange rate, on the other hand, will have the opposite effect. If all this is the case, will a fall in the exchange rate therefore be good for our international trade position? Not necessarily. A price rise will reduce demand, but by how much? What, for example, would happen to revenue if a 20% price increase resulted in only a 20% fall in quantity demanded? The **Marshall Lerner Condition** says that it depends on how responsive to changes in price people are. Although the price of Japanese cars may increase, people may still carry on buying them. Similarly, although the price of UK exports may fall, if people are convinced that they are rubbish, they will still not buy them. Usually, a fall in the exchange rate will reduce imports and increase exports, but things might get worse before they get better. This is because increased demand for exports will take a while to feed through the chain of ordering, manufacture and delivery, whereas more will be paid for imports *immediately*. This is called the **J Curve Effect** – see Figure 27.3.

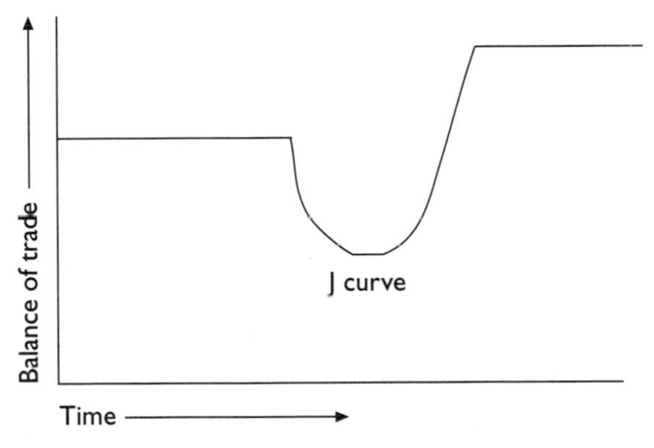

Figure 27.3 The J Curve Effect

Ministers told not to let pound slump further

The government must prevent sterling from falling from current levels or run the risk that inflation will rise above the 4 per cent official target. The more interest rates are lowered, to stimulate recovery, the greater the risk that they will have to be raised. Exports are expected to do well over the next two years, helped by the devaluation, but imports will continue at a high level, both in volume and in price terms.

(The Times, 15 February 1993)

Think! Why might prices rise if the pound falls 'from current levels'? Given the information you have read so far, why might exports do well after a devaluation, while imports 'continue at a high level'?

Fixed and floating exchange rates

Although the main influences on exchange rates are supply and demand, governments too can influence the value of a currency. At its extreme, this involves deciding on a particular value and then adopting measures to keep the currency at that level. How is this done?

Earlier in the chapter, we saw that, fundamentally, an exchange rate is determined by the demand in foreign countries for a country's goods and services. Governments find it difficult to influence this. However, we have seen that the exchange rate can also be influenced by interest rates: raising the interest rate will generally increase the demand for a currency and therefore increase its price.

Furthermore, from time to time, governments have entered into agreements where they are obliged to adopt measures that will keep the value of their currency at a particular level – i.e. at a **fixed exchange rate**. The advantage of a fixed exchange rate is that businesses can then make predictions about the prices of both their imports (for buying raw materials) and their exports (for sales). This is very important, as a company importing cars will have to pay more for the imports if the currency depreciates (falls in value). The company will try to pass these increased costs on to its customers by increasing prices. This will reduce the company's sales and therefore its profits. So, an importer loses out if the currency depreciates. On the other hand, exporters will gain, as their products will be cheaper in the foreign market and so their sales will increase. However, an *appreciation* of the currency (an increase in value) will have the opposite effect for exporters. Therefore, businesses generally prefer the exchange rate to remain stable.

A disadvantage of fixed exchange rates is that a country may need to run a high interest rate, making borrowing very expensive and discouraging investment, in order to keep the exchange fixed.

The alternative is to allow the exchange rate to float, i.e. the government does not worry about the exchange rate when choosing policies. A currency may indeed be left completely free to find its price on the basis of supply and demand in the market. This is called **clean floating**. Usually, however, a government will take some interest in the value of a currency if only to stop large fluctuations from day to day. Here, the government may intervene by using the central bank to buy or sell pounds. This is known as a **managed float** or **dirty floating**.

The advantages and disadvantages of a floating exchange rate are the opposite to those for a fixed rate. So, what are they?

The European Monetary System

The Exchange Rate Mechanism (ERM) of the European Monetary System (EMS) was set up by the countries of the European Community in 1979. The UK refused to join until 1990. The ERM is a **semi-fixed** exchange-rate system. In a fixed system, governments agree to adopt policies that will keep their currency 'pegged' to a specific exchange rate against other currencies. In the ERM, a currency only has to stay within a *band* around a fixed point. They can fluctuate around that fixed point (for the UK from 1990–92, by 6% either way), but if the currency is going too high, the government must take action to reduce its value, and if it is going too low, it must take action to increase its value. In August 1993, the 6% and 2.25% bands were widened to 15% for all ERM currencies except the Dutch guilder.

Black Wednesday?

The main problem with fixing your exchange rate to the currency of another country is that an important factor in deciding the exchange rate is the level of interest rates. If interest rates were all the same, then financial institutions would rather keep their money in a country with a record of low inflation so that it would maintain its value. The UK does not have a record of low inflation, and so to persuade financial institutions to keep money in the UK, a higher rate of interest must be offered than that in, say, Germany.

Throughout the summer of 1992, it was reported that the interest rates needed to maintain the exchange of the pound against the Deutsche Mark were far too high because the UK was suffering a recession whilst Germany's problem was inflation. On Wednesday 17 September, foreign-currency dealers began to sell pounds in the expectation that interest rates would soon have to fall. The Bank of England, assisted by other European central banks, started to sell its currency reserves to buy pounds. However, pounds were being sold more quickly than they could be bought. This continued until 11 am when the Bank of England announced that it would raise interest rates from 10% to 12%. Nobody believed that this would last, and the pound continued to be sold. At 2.15 pm, the interest rate was raised to 15%, and when even this didn't work, the government announced that the pound was leaving the ERM.

In the next few weeks, the exchange rate fell by around 20% against the Deutsche Mark, and over the next few months interest rates were reduced to 6%. The depreciation of the pound led to increased demand for UK exports, while the fall in interest rates led to increased demand in the UK home market.

So, was it 'Black Wednesday' after all? Some people indeed refer to it as 'White Wednesday'. What do *you* think? Divide a page into two columns. In the left-hand column, put a heading 'Black Wednesday' and in the right, write 'White Wednesday'. Under 'Black Wednesday', write all the disadvantages you can think of connected with the UK's withdrawal from the ERM. Under 'White Wednesday', list all the advantages that have come about.

A single currency for Europe?

On 1 January 1993, a **Single Market** was established throughout the European Community. (Many businesses might ask: how can you have a single market with so many different currencies?) The aim of the Single Market was to make it as easy for someone in Manchester to buy a product produced in Milan as it is for someone in Los Angeles, California to buy something produced in Houston, Texas: the current problem is that Manchester uses pounds sterling whilst Milan uses Italian lira, whereas in both California and Texas, the US dollar is the currency used. What's more, if you go on holiday to another European country, you are faced with the problem of how to take foreign money. If you buy foreign currency from a bank, you will be charged **commission**, which is often around 2–5%. Now imagine that you are a business dealing in millions of pounds. Paying banks for foreign exchange would then be very expensive. A **single currency** would solve not only the problem of cost but also the problem of unpredictability of appreciations and depreciations discussed earlier.

However, who would control a single currency for Europe? In the UK, the supply of money is affected by interest rates which are put up or down by the Chancellor of the Exchequer. The Chancellor acts on behalf of the UK government and is accountable to the electorate, which means that the government can be voted out if the population of the country dislikes its policies. Could all the finance ministers of the European Union get together to fix interest rates throughout Europe? This, however, would make quick decisions almost impossible. A more likely system is the German system of an independent **Central Bank** controlling European interest rates, but where then is the democratic control?

Another problem with the single currency might arise if one country is suffering from a lack of demand so that there is high unemployment, whilst another country has plenty of demand leading to inflation. Should European interest rates then go up or down?

Summary

Exchange rates are the price of one currency when bought with another. Exchange rates can be fixed or floating. Exchange rates are determined by supply and demand.

Changes in exchange rates result in big changes in costs and revenue for businesses. Amongst member countries of the European Union, there are moves to adopt a single currency.

chapter 27

MAKES YOU THINK!

1 A Jaguar car is sold for £25,000. What will be its price in the USA (the biggest market for Jaguars) at the following exchange rates:

(a) £1 = $2.50
(b) £1 = $2.00
(c) £1 = $1.50
(d) £1 = $1.00?

At which of these exchange rates would Americans be mostly likely to buy Jaguars?

2 You go on holiday to France. Your hotel bill comes to 1,500 francs. If the exchange rate is:

(a) £1 = FF11
(b) £1 = FF10
(c) £1 = FF9
(d) £1 = FF8

how much money in pounds will you need to change to pay your bill?

3 What is likely to happen to the exchange rate of the pound against the Deutsche Mark in each of the following situations?

(a) Volkswagen produces a new car that is highly desirable, very reliable and rather cheap
(b) Germany raises its rate of interest
(c) The English Tourist Board carries out a highly successful advertising campaign in Germany.

The European Union

In 1957, six countries (France, West Germany, Italy, Belgium, Luxembourg and the Netherlands) signed the Treaty of Rome which set out a programme to reduce the following hindrances to free trade in Europe:

- the imposition of tariffs and the restricted movement of goods
- the inability of workers to move freely to jobs in other countries
- the restrictions placed on selling services
- the restrictions on the free movement of capital
- the distortion of competition
- the difference in laws which prevent a common market
- the varying levels of tax such as VAT

By 1968, the free trade area had established a **customs union**, but it took until 1 January 1993 for a Single Market to be proclaimed. In the meantime, the original six countries had been joined by Denmark, Ireland and the United Kingdom (in 1973); Greece (in 1981); and Portugal and Spain (in 1986). Austria, Sweden and Finland joined in 1995. In 1992, the Treaty of Maastricht changed the European Community into the European Union, of which all nationals of the member states became citizens (all Britons are now citizens of the Union as well as of the United Kingdom). The Treaty also set out a timetable to achieve a single currency by the end of the century. This European Union came into official existence on 1 November 1993, following the coming into force of the Maastricht Treaty, but with most countries still unsure of what it should be called. The European Union officially extended the European Community, which in turn was the more up-to-date name for the European Economic Community, itself an improvement on the original unofficial but more popular term, the Common Market.

Does it make any difference to you whether the organisation is called the European Economic Community, the European Community or the European Union? Why does it matter to governments as to which term is used?

A free trade area

A **free trade area** is created when a group of countries decides that there should be no trade barriers (e.g. tariffs or quotas) between them. They do this so that they may all benefit from **free trade**, and so that they may each buy the most efficiently produced goods. On the other hand, each country in this area maintains quotas and tariffs on goods coming from outside the free trade area.

Europe extends free trade area

The world's biggest free trade market, from the Arctic to the Mediterranean, was born at midnight last night as the European Community linked up with five members of the European Free Trade Association (Efta). The European Economic Area (EEA) will extend the EC's single market to Austria, Finland, Iceland, Norway and Sweden, setting the stage for an

> **enlarged EC next year. Liechtenstein hopes to join after it has renegotiated its customs agreement with Switzerland, whose voters rejected taking part in the market.**
>
> **The North American Free Trade Agreement (Nafta) linking America, Canada and Mexico also came into force last night. Nafta covers a land area nearly five times that of the EEA, but the EEA has 372 million consumers against Nafta's 360 million and a greater gross domestic product.**

(The Times, 1 January 1994)

A customs union

Suppose that three countries, A, B and C, form a free trade area, and that they each impose tariffs on imports from outside the area: in country A, the tariff on imports is 10%, in country B it is 25%, and in country C it is 30%. Suppose that country D, which lies outside the free trade area, wants to sell something to somebody in country C. The sensible course of action for country D is to set up a company in country A, export to that company, thus paying only the 10% tariff, and then re-export to country C with no tariff charged. The effect is that country C gains no taxes whilst country A with the lowest tariffs gains all the tax that should go to country C. (See Figure 28.1.)

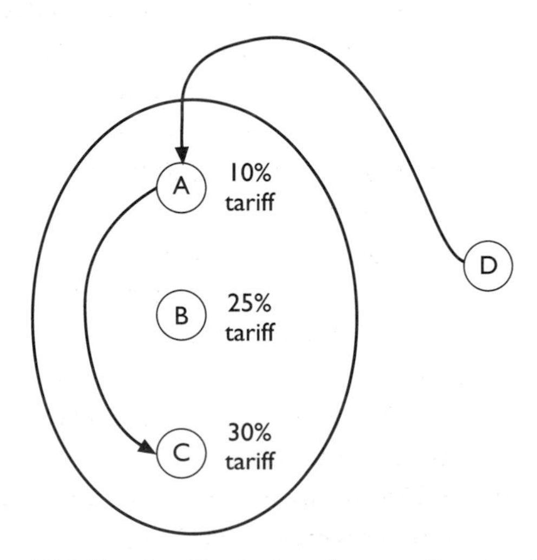

Figure 28.1 Country D's strategy for exporting to a free trade area

An answer to this strategy would be to agree on a common tariff, but what should that tariff be and how could it be changed? Each country in the free trade area would have to agree to giving up its right to set its own level of tax on imports. Therefore, each country would give up some of its own **sovereignty** (i.e. its absolute right to make laws) to an institution that is now made up of several countries.

A common or single market

When such a customs union exists, there are still other barriers to the complete freedom of trade between members of a group. If the aim is to make it as easy to sell something made in one country to a person in another country as it is to sell it to someone else in the original country, then further barriers need to be removed, such as the following:

- Removing physical frontiers such as border checks on people and goods
- Establishing common safety standards
- The recognition of the same professional qualifications in each country
- Accepting **tenders** (bids) for contracts in the public sector from anywhere in the union
- Bringing together tax rates on goods
- Common environmental policies

The institutions of the European Union

It has already been said that in order to make decisions which apply to all the member countries of a union, special bodies need to be created. In the European Union (EU), the following institutions have been set up:

The Council of Ministers

This is the decision-making body of the EU. It is the only institution that can make laws. The Council consists of the relevant minister from each national government. So, if agriculture is being discussed, then the UK Agriculture Minister attends, and when more general matters are being discussed, the Foreign Secretary attends.

At least once every six months, the heads of government meet to decide on major issues. The Council is chaired by each country in turn for six months.

The Commission

This is the civil service of the European Union, responsible for proposing ideas to the Council of Ministers and for ensuring that the ministers' decisions are acted upon. The Commission is based in Brussels and is headed by a president who is chosen by the heads of government. Appointments of **commissioners**, who head the various departments of the Commission, are made by governments, but these must also be approved by the European Parliament. Commissioners promise to work for the joint interests of the whole EU rather than for just their individual countries.

Old hands to lead Santer team for Europe

The current salary of a European commissioner is equivalent to about £100,000 per annum, taxed at a low preferential rate. Each has an official car and a chauffeur.

The commissioners are:

Jacques Santer (Luxembourg): President of the Commission; overall responsibility for common foreign and security policy, and economic and monetary union;

Hans van den Broek (The Netherlands): external relations with Central and Eastern Europe, the Baltic republics and the states of the former Soviet Union; operational responsibility for foreign and security policy;

Manuel Marin (Spain): external relations with the southern Mediterranean, Middle East, parts of the Far East and Latin America;

Sir Leon Brittan (UK): foreign trade and external relations with countries of Organisation for Economic Development and Co-operation, plus parts of Asia;

Joao de Deus Pinheiro (Portugal): external relations with Africa, Caribbean and Pacific;

Yves-Thibault de Silguy (France): economic affairs;

Mario Monti (Italy): internal market, financial service, customs and tax;

Karel van Miert (Belgium): competition;
Martin Bangemann (Germany): industry, technology;
Padraig Flynn (Ireland): social affairs;
Marcelino Oreja (Spain): relations with European Parliament, culture and media;
Edith Cresson (France): research and development, education;
Ritt Bjerregaard (Denmark): environment, nuclear safety;
Monika Wulf-Mathies (Germany): regional policy;
Neil Kinnock (UK): transport;
Emma Bonino (Italy): consumer affairs;
Christos Papoutsis (Greece): atomic energy, small and medium-sized companies, and tourism;
Thorvald Stoltenberg (Norway): fisheries;
Anita Gradin (Sweden): interior and judicial affairs;
Franz Fischler (Austria): agriculture;
Erkki Liikanen (Finland); budget, personnel and administration.

(The Times, 31 October 1994)

The European Parliament

This is the only directly elected institution in the European Union. **Euro MPs** (MEPs) are elected for five years, and they represent their local constituency and their political party rather than their country. Although their power is quite limited, the Parliament does have the right both to reject the EU's budget and to reject members of the Commission.

The European Parliament is based in Brussels, but holds its main meetings for one week a month in Strasbourg.

The European Court of Justice

This meets in the Hague, and its job is to ensure that European law is followed. It can punish, by fines, individuals, companies or governments. It is the highest court on all matters of EU law.

Governments favouring their national airlines led to disputes, where small airlines took other airlines, governments or the Commission to the European Court to enforce rules of free competition.

The European Court of Justice is sometimes confused with the European Court of Human Rights based in Strasbourg. However, the two Courts have absolutely no connection. The Human Rights Court is part of the **Council of Europe** which is a cultural, social and educational body with a membership that is both wider and older than that of the European Union.

Aims of the European Union

The original objective of the EU was to increase the prosperity of its inhabitants by allowing them to get the benefits of the most efficient production in Europe – wherever that may be. As always in economics, it is very difficult to know exactly how successful the EU has been in meeting its aim because we don't know what things would have been like if the EU had never existed. However, the *Lloyds Bank Bulletin* has estimated that the UK has experienced an extra

0.5% of extra economic activity each year on average as a result of membership. Over time, the cumulative effect of this extra activity is very large, and this is largely due to the export market provided by membership.

Criticisms of the European Union

Many people in the UK are very critical of the EU. Most accept the benefits of a free trade area but they worry about the EU being involved in social, regional and transport policy, monopolies and the environment. Since the first Customs Union, greater decision-making powers have been given up by national governments to Brussels. This has led to a reaction against centralising power in Brussels, which in turn has led to the adoption of the idea of **subsidiarity**, i.e. that decisions should be made as close as possible to the area to which they apply, so that, for example, national governments decide how much to spend on defence whilst local government controls refuse collection.

Future developments

The two most important future developments being discussed are:

1 the enlargement of the EU to include the countries of Central and Eastern Europe;
2 the creation of a single currency.

The newly democratised countries of Central and Eastern Europe such as Hungary, the Czech Republic and Poland are anxious to join, but by the mid-1990s they were a lot poorer than even the poorest of the existing members (Greece and Portugal), although this situation is rapidly changing.

Meanwhile, plans to have a single currency for use in all EU countries are proceeding, much to the anguish of many British politicians (see Chapter 27).

Summary

The European Union comprises: France, Germany, Italy, the UK, the Netherlands, Belgium, Luxembourg, Denmark, Greece, Spain, Portugal, Ireland, Austria, Sweden and Finland.

The EU has eradicated trade barriers between member states, and has introduced the free movement of people, goods and money between its members. It is run by institutions which contain representatives, from each country, who work for the interests of the whole Union.

Many people in the UK worry about the loss of sovereignty (i.e. the loss of the right of the British Parliament to make any laws it wishes) as more power is given to EU institutions.

1 Does a country within the European Union have less sovereignty than one outside it?
2 Is the case for a single currency in Europe any different from the case for a single currency for England and Scotland or for the USA?
3 When should the countries of Central and Eastern Europe be allowed to join the EU? What would be the effects of their joining?

Chapter 29

Economic development

The houses are occupied from cellar to garret, filthy within and without, and their appearance is such that no human being could possibly wish to live in them. But all this is nothing in comparison with the dwellings in the narrow courts, and alleys between the streets, entered by covered passages between the houses, in which the filth and tottering ruins surpass all description. Scarcely a whole window-pane can be found, the walls are crumbling, door frames are loose and broken, doors of old boards nailed together, or altogether wanting in this thieves' quarter, where no doors are needed, there being nothing to steal. Heaps of garbage and ashes lie in all directions, and the foul liquids emptied before the doors gather in stinking pools. Here the poorest of the poor, the worst paid workers with thieves and the victims of prostitution indiscriminately huddle together.

This is not a description of a Third World shanty town. It is London in the middle of the nineteenth century. The source is Frederick Engels' *The Condition of the English Working Class*. How far has the country developed in 150 years?

The meaning of First and Third World

Some economists classify countries into either the First, Second or Third Worlds. These definitions are oversimplistic and need to be treated with care, but they do allow us to make broad generalisations:

- **First World** countries comprise that small group of industrialised countries to be found in Western Europe, North America, Australia, New Zealand and Japan. Other names to describe the same group are: the West, **industrialised countries**, **developed countries** or the North (as these countries are mainly found in the Northern Hemisphere)
- **Second World** countries include Russia and the countries of East and Central Europe that were under communist forms of government until 1989/90; but some are also found in the North. Although these countries are industrialised, their per-capita gross domestic product is well below the per-capita GDP of First World countries
- **Third World** countries contain around three-quarters of the world's population. This category describes the countries of Africa, Asia and South and Central America. Within the vast number of countries involved here, there is great variation. Indeed, even within countries themselves there is often a considerable difference between the living standards of the richest and the poorest. In the Republic of South Africa, the white minority enjoy a

First World standard of living, and whilst some of the black population are now able to reach similar lifestyles, the vast majority of black people still live in great poverty

There are other countries, such as Singapore or South Korea, that are known as **Newly Industrialised Countries** (NICs). This phrase describes the richest of the Third World nations – i.e. those that have recently developed an industrial base similar to those found in the West. It is questionable whether these countries are still part of the Third World, but as they have only recently developed an industrial base, their GDP per capita is still low compared to the First World.

Although – as has been said – the description 'Third World' is far too simplistic, there are some basic problems that these **developing countries** do share.

Problems faced by developing countries

Low income

The **World Bank** (the International Bank for Reconstruction and Development (IBRD)) defines countries by their GNP per capita. It finds the classifications of 'low income', 'middle income' and 'high income' useful. High-income countries generally correspond to the First World. There are considerable differences between incomes of the richest and poorest countries in each category, but Table 29.1 illustrates that there are also clear differences *between* these categories. Remember that although GNP per capita is a very useful indicator as to the comparative poverty or wealth of a country, it is limited in the help it can give us because it is only an average figure and there are often wide differences in wealth within countries. In the UK, we know that some people's income was much more than $16,550, and that, on the other hand, many people in the population – e.g. children – receive no income at all.

Table 29.1 Average income (GNP per capita) of 12 countries, 1990 ($US)

High-income countries	
Switzerland	**33,610**
USA	**22,240**
UK	**16,550**
Spain	**12,450**
Middle-income countries	
Uruguay	**2,840**
Malaysia	**2,530**
Botswana	**2,520**
Philippines	**730**
Low-income countries	
India	**330**
China	**370**
Bangladesh	**220**
Ethiopia	**120**

(IBRD World Development Report 1993)

Measures of the standard of living

National income (using per-capita GNP figures) is a good indication of living standards (see again Chapter 24). In the First World, however, it is often suggested that an increase in national income will not necessarily increase living standards. Think: somebody earns £50,000 a year in return for working 70 hours a week. They are then offered the chance to earn an extra £1,000 a year in return for working an extra 5 hours a week. What will be more valuable to the worker, £1,000 or 5 hours a week of leisure time? The same principle can be applied on a national scale: increased wealth may be available to a country only in exchange for working longer and harder, dying younger etc. Therefore, a rich industrialised country may wish to debate the desirability of further economic growth.

However, a Third World country with a very low national income will not be able to afford the luxury of such a debate. Moreover, such a country will have some further urgent issues of its own to address.

Life expectancy

This will generally be short in Third World countries – though, as Table 29.2 suggests, not always.

Table 29.2 A comparison of GNP per capita against life expectancy, 1991

Country	GNP per capita ($US)	Life expectancy
Mozambique	80	47
Nigeria	340	52
Zimbabwe	650	60
Mexico	3,030	70
China	370	69
Costa Rica	1,850	76
Brazil	2,940	66
Denmark	23,700	75

(IBRD World Development Report 1993, Table 1)

Infant mortality

This is another indicator of poor standards of living. The **infant mortality rate** is the number of babies who do not survive to 1 year of age out of every 1,000 live births. Table 29.3 shows that in Denmark, a rich First World country, 8 babies in every 1,000 (0.8%) die before reaching the age of 1, whilst in Mozambique almost 15% of babies never make it to their first birthday.

Table 29.3 A comparison of GNP per capita against infant mortality rates, 1991

Country	GNP per capita ($US)	Infant mortality
Mozambique	80	149
Nigeria	340	85
Zimbabwe	650	48
Mexico	3,030	36
Denmark	23,700	8

(Source as above)

Adult illiteracy

Here is another key indicator of low living standards. Again, there is a strong connection between GNP per capita and the adult illiteracy rate (see Table 29.4). However, education may well be a priority for a Third World country, but it will obviously come further down a list than feeding the population.

Table 29.4 A comparison of GNP per capita against adult illiteracy

Country	GNP per capita ($US)	Adult illiteracy (%)	
		Female	Male
Mozambique	80	79	67
Nigeria	340	61	49
Zimbabwe	650	40	33
Mexico	3,030	15	13
Denmark	23,700	Almost non-existent	

(IBRD World Development Report 1993, Table 28)

Poor health

This is another characteristic of the populations of Third World countries. It is difficult to measure health, but the infant mortality rates and life expectancies already looked at above are helpful indicators. Another useful statistic is the number of patients per doctor. Compare the population-per-doctor ratio in the Third World and First World countries shown in Table 29.5.

Table 29.5 Population per physician, 1990

Burkina Faso	57,320	Japan	610
Ethiopia	32,650	Canada	450
Kenya	10,130	Austria	230

(Source as above)

High population growth

This is yet another issue concerning Third World countries. I do not say 'problem', because it is all too easy to think of people as a problem. If the Queen of England has the right to have four children, then a poor African woman surely has the same right. However, women in the West have much more of a choice as to whether to have children. They can make use of widely available contraceptives or choose to forgo sex. Western women are generally much more empowered to make choices in their life than are their sisters in the Third World. Education about family planning allows Western women to have some say over their lives.

More than three-quarters of the world's population lives in the Third World, and the population growth here is so high that it is twice that in the West. This has an effect on the age structure. About one-third of the population of Third World countries is under 15 years of age, compared to one-fifth in First World countries. This means that the **dependency burden** (the ratio of nonworkers to workers) is far greater in the Third World. The evidence from the First World suggests, indeed, that as countries grow richer, the size of families decreases.

One of the main reasons for large families in the Third World is that people can only guarantee being looked after in old age by having a large enough number of children to ensure that some will survive and look after their parents when they can no longer work: Third World countries cannot afford pensions and old peoples' homes.

Primary production

This form of production holds many Third World countries captive, and unfortunately, the production of raw materials earns very little money. It is the manufacturing of those raw materials into something more useful that 'adds value', and Third World countries often lack the skills and money needed for investment into such manufacturing. Furthermore, where Third World countries *are* able to produce manufactured goods, First World countries often impose tariffs which make it difficult to sell those goods in the West.

Low labour productivity

This is associated with the heavy reliance on primary production of Third World countries, and again, it is part of a trap that is difficult to break out of. Workers are paid very little for their labour, which means that they have no surplus money to save. Money for investment comes from savings, and with a low level of saving there is little money to invest in capital or machinery. There is also little money for taxes to pay for a good education system, and this leads to low levels of **human capital**. A lack of education, a lack of good health and a lack of capital investment are all results of low labour productivity, and in turn they all *lead* to low levels of productivity; so it is a real trap, as Figure 29.1 illustrates.

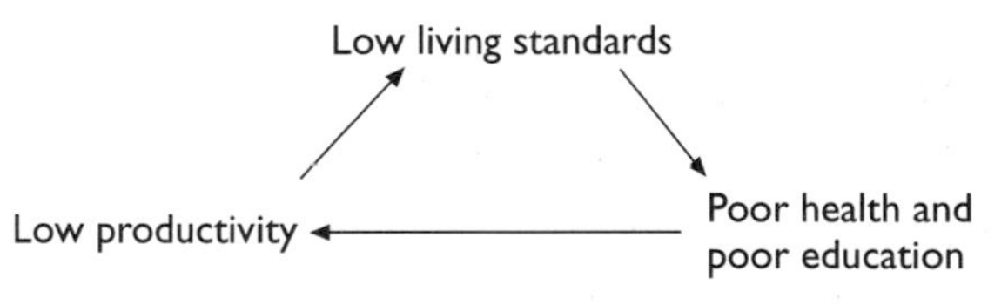

Figure 29.1 The Third World poverty trap

Third World debt

During the 1970s, Western banks found that they had lots of money available for lending. Interest rates were low, and Third World countries were encouraged to take out long-term loans. During the 1980s, the situation in the West changed, and interest rates rose dramatically in an effort to curb inflation. Third World countries that had taken out loans at low rates of interest now found that they had to repay very high rates of

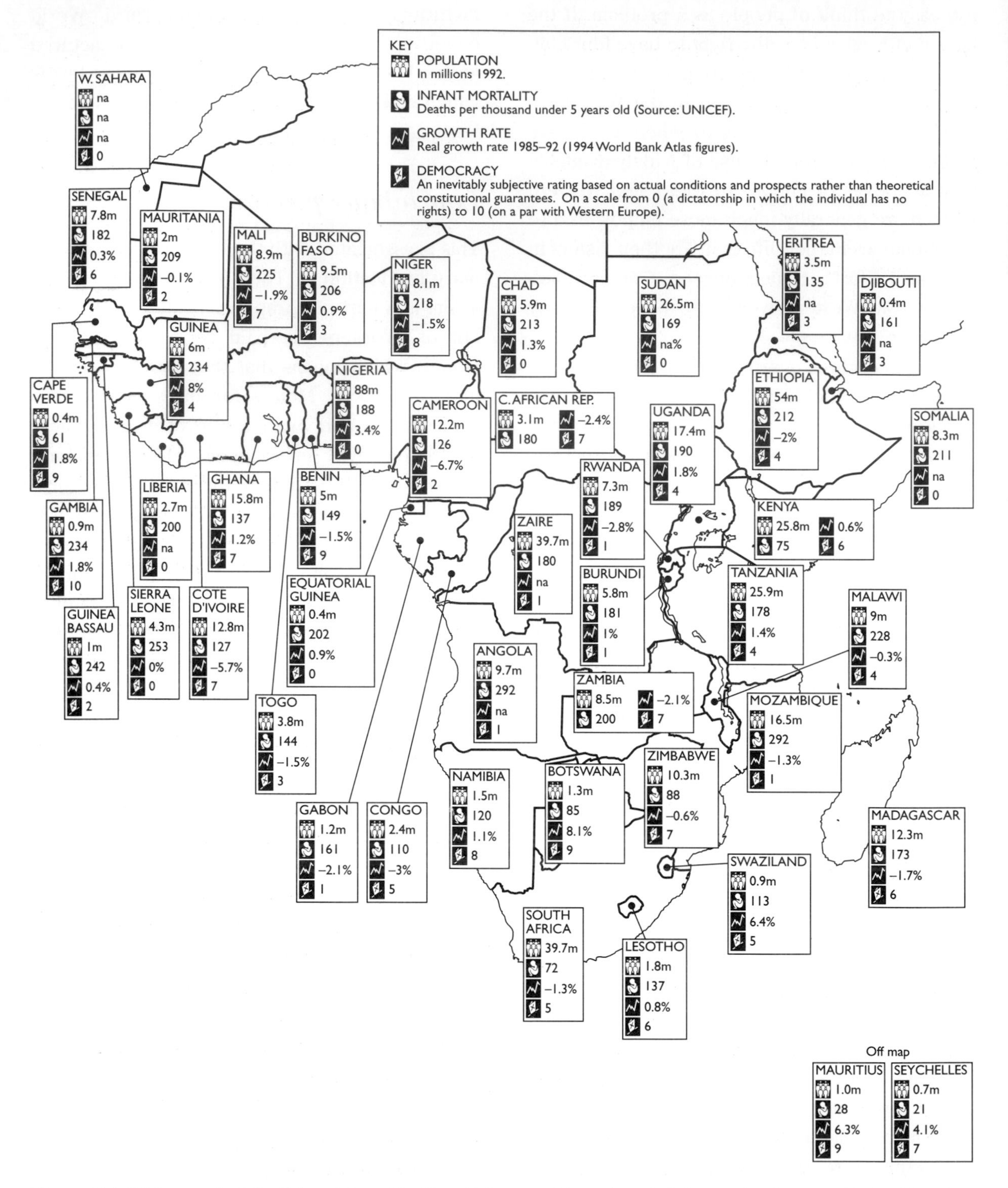

Figure 29.2 'Africa south of the Sahara' from The New Africa: a guide to the sub-Saharan Continent, by Richard Dowden, *Independent on Sunday,* 13 March 1994

interest. More and more, their production was diverted to paying off this interest rather than using the money for development projects such as improving education, health or technology.

Foreign aid from the First World to the Third World

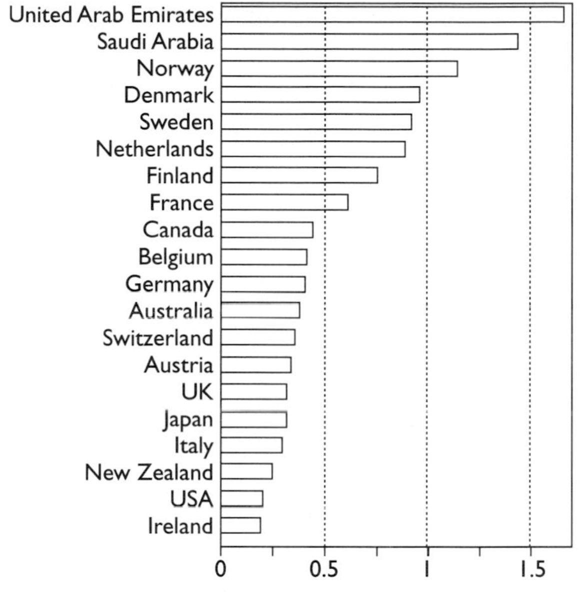

Figure 29.3 Official development assistance as a percentage of the donor's GNP (IBRD World Development Report 1993)

Foreign aid (see Figure 29.2) can take one of the following forms:

- **Grants** are the most generous form of aid. Here, a donor country might pay for a development project in a Third World country. The former may offer free technical advice, or it might pay for students from the latter to gain free university education in the Western country
- **Loans** are a common form of aid. However, as we have seen, loans may be granted at the market rate of interest, and so no real favours are being done. **Soft loans**, on the other hand, carry a lower rate of interest than do normal commercial loans
- **Tied aid** is a grant or a loan that is only given if the money is then used to purchase goods or services from the country giving the grant or loan. The UK, for example, has a policy of using its foreign aid budget to boost British exports
- **Bilateral** and **multilateral aid** describe whether the aid is being given by one country or by a group of countries. A UK loan to Zimbabwe would be bilateral aid, whereas multilateral aid is given by agencies such as UN bodies and the World Bank. Whilst multilateral aid is generally not tied, bilateral aid is usually dependent on purchases being made from the donating country.

Of course, a lot of aid is unofficial and is provided by **Non-Governmental Organisations** (NGOs). Some well-known NGOs are Oxfam, Christian Aid, Cafod and Action Aid. Members of the Salvation Army in First World countries have a special service once a year called a **self-denial alter service**. Salvationists are encouraged to give one week's salary in this alter service, the entire collection going directly to projects in the Third World.

We operate a project offering supplementary reading and writing lessons for 90 street children. Homeless children are a big problem in Vita dos Pescadores. Many youngsters come from the north of Brazil where there has been a prolonged drought. Their parents cannot afford rent and shanty towns just grow and grow. Many Salvationists and friends from Sweden, Norway and Canada provide sponsorship for the children.

(Captain Margaret England, Salvationist, 18 March 1995. Captain Margaret England is a British Salvation Army officer who has been working in Brazil for the last ten years. She used to be a school teacher in England. The

Salvation Army is one of many Christian churches who have members working to alleviate suffering in the Third World.)

What do you think motivates people to choose to work for charities?

The terms of trade

The last 20 years have seen periods of very high inflation in developed countries. This has meant that Third World countries have had to find more cash to pay for the same amount of imports from First World countries. At the same time, large First World companies have used their purchasing power to hold down the price of commodities such as coffee, tea and minerals. As a result, Third World countries have had to devote ever-larger areas of land and increasing resources to exports of **cash crops** in order to afford a limited supply of imports. This has left fewer resources available to feed the population and to invest in health, education and general progress.

The terms of trade (see Chapter 26) are:

$$\frac{\text{index of export prices}}{\text{index of import prices}} \times 100$$

Since export prices have stayed much the same whilst import prices have risen greatly, we can say that the terms of trade for Third World countries has worsened considerably.

Sweeping reforms in the World Bank were called for yesterday by Christian Aid, which accused it of wastefulness and causing widespread social and environmental damage in the Third World . . .

A report from Christian Aid, 'Who Runs The World?', published to coincide with the Bank's fiftieth anniversary, says structural adjustment programmes, introduced in response to the Third World debt crisis, have produced massive unemployment, the collapse of health and education systems, cultural disintegration and severe soil erosion and deforestation.

Despite widening the poverty gap both within developing countries and between the developing and the industrialised world, the programmes have not solved the crisis, according to the report. Third World debt continues to grow and the bank and the International Monetary Fund receive more than they hand out.

The charity is launching a campaign aimed at opening the bank to public scrutiny and promoting environmentally friendly and 'people-based' alternatives to what it regards as the Bank's obsession with failed free-market orthodoxies. Taxpayers (British) paid £239 million to the bank and the IMF last year, 13 per cent of its aid budget.

(The Independent, 20 July 1994)

Newly Industrialised Countries

As already mentioned, some countries, notably countries in East Asia such as Hong Kong, South Korea, Singapore and Taiwan, are growing very rapidly.

The four Asian dragons – Hong Kong, South Korea, Singapore and Taiwan – also enjoyed rapid expansion, with average increases in their GDPs of 6–9%.

(The Economist, 18 September 1993)

These Newly Industrialised Countries have managed to achieve a level of prosperity which has allowed their governments to direct money into investment and education. This was only achieved when their agriculture industries became so productive that people could leave the land and work in the manufacturing industry instead – as happened in the West 150–200 years ago. The secret here is the production of a surplus. In the UK, only 2% of the workforce is employed in agriculture. However, it produces enough food for everyone else, leaving 98% of the workforce free to produce other goods and services. In Germany, only 2% of GDP comes from agriculture, whilst in Thailand the figure is 12%; but Uganda, on the other hand, is more characteristic of a Third World country, for here 67% of GDP comes from agriculture.

However, although Newly Industrialised Countries are investing heavily in industry and their standard of living is increasing rapidly, they are still poor compared with Western countries. This means that businesses producing in these countries face low labour costs (wages), and so goods can be produced cheaply. Western countries are now very concerned that the pay and conditions of workers in the West mean that labour costs make goods produced in Western Europe too expensive. It is argued that this is a major reason for high levels of unemployment in the European Union in the 1990s.

Consider these questions:

1 Is the answer to unemployment in the European Union to impose quotas and tariffs on goods produced in Newly Industrialised Countries?
2 When you are buying electrical equipment (like a CD player or a TV), do you prefer the price to be high or low?
3 What effect do quotas and tariffs have on the price of your electrical equipment?

Summary

Economic growth in very poor countries is called development. Characteristics of Third World or developing countries include: low income, low life expectancy, high infant mortality rates, high levels of adult illiteracy, poor standards of health, high levels of population growth, a high proportion of the population involved in primary production, especially agriculture, and low levels of labour productivity.

Foreign aid is given by First World countries to Third World countries, but its effectiveness is questionable.

The terms of trade of Third World countries have worsened in the last 20 years, but Newly Industrialised Countries have nonetheless managed to achieve high levels of economic growth, and their success is seen as a threat to First World countries.

A final word

In the 1970s, an international commission headed by the former West German Chancellor Billy Brandt published a report recommending that Western industrialised countries (i.e. generally the Northern Hemisphere) take action to promote economic development in the Southern Hemisphere, claiming that this would actually serve the interests of the North. Since then, projects such as 'Band Aid' and responses to appeals from charities have shown that people can be moved to give money and time for causes that influence them emotionally, to act in ways that are altruistic. Economics finds difficulty in taking on board **altruism**, and therefore the subject cannot *entirely* explain the behaviour of individuals and groups. As we saw at the beginning of this book, economics can offer theories to explain how people are likely to act, but it's nonetheless a very inexact science!

chapter 29

MAKES YOU THINK!

1 Using the information in this chapter, draw up two lists. On one, put countries in order of GDP per capita, and on the other put countries in order of life expectancy. What similarities and differences do you discover? Do the results surprise you?

2 (a) What was the average growth rate for all sub-Saharan African countries in the period 1985–92?
  (b) Is there any connection between population size, infant mortality and growth rate?

3 Find out about what is involved in sponsoring a child in a Third World country. You may like to take this on as a group, whilst learning more about the economy of that country. Possible contacts are: Action Aid, Oxfam, Tear Fund, or your local Salvation Army centre.

Index